Contemporary Discourse
in the Field of
ASTRONOMY ™

How Life on Earth Is Affected by Earth's Unique Placement and Orientation in Our Solar System

An Anthology of Current Thought

Edited by Eric M. Monier, Ph.D.

The Rosen Publishing Group, Inc., New York

Published in 2006 by The Rosen Publishing Group, Inc.
29 East 21st Street, New York, NY 10010

First Edition

Library of Congress Cataloging-in-Publication Data

How life on earth is affected by earth's unique placement and orientation in our solar system: an anthology of current thought/edited by Eric M. Monier.—1st ed.
    p. cm.—(Contemporary discourse in the field of astronomy)
Includes bibliographical references and index.
ISBN 1-4042-0392-3 (library binding)
1. Solar system—Origin. 2. Earth—Origin.
I. Monier, Eric. II. Series.
QB503.H69 2005
523.2—dc22

                                        2004026364

Manufactured in the United States of America

On the cover: Bottom right: The nine planets. Bottom left: Galileo Galilei. Center left: The Dumbell Nebula. Top right: Solar flares.

CONTENTS

Introduction

About 4.6 billion years ago, a cold cloud of gas and dust began to form. This cloud peacefully occupied the galactic real estate that was to become our solar system. It was left behind by previous generations of stars destroyed in supernova explosions. It orbited the Milky Way once every 225 million years and also rotated slowly on its own axis. One day, something—maybe a supernova explosion somewhere nearby in the galaxy—unleashed a shock wave that passed through the cloud. This shock wave set in motion the chain of events that ultimately led to the formation of our solar system, Earth, and human beings, who today are asking questions about how the universe and life came to be.

The disturbance caused the gravity of the cloud to overcome the weak gas pressure generated by the cloud's cold interior. As the cloud collapsed under its gravity, it rotated faster and faster, obeying the conservation of angular momentum, the same principle that causes an ice skater to spin faster as he or she draws in his or her arms. The spinning flattened the cloud, like pizza dough when a chef twirls it in the air. The collapsing cloud also heated up as its potential, or stored, gravitational energy was steadily converted into kinetic energy, the energy of motion. This heating effect accelerated the atoms and molecules within.

Most of the gas ended up in the center, which was growing increasingly hot and dense. The remainder stretched out in a disk about twice the size of Pluto's orbit today. When the core of this "solar nebula" reached a temperature of millions of degrees and the enormous pressure necessary for fusion to begin, our Sun "turned on," and its main sequence lifetime began.

Meanwhile, the nebula surrounding the forming Sun cooled and the gases in it began condensing out into grains that stuck to each other like snowflakes on a snowball. In the inner regions of the nebula, the temperature was still high enough that only rocky materials and metals took solid form. Ices—including water, ammonia, and methane—were left to form in the colder regions beyond the orbit of Mars. Within roughly 30 million years, these initial bits of rock and ice had combined to form the planets, moons, asteroids, and comets we see today.

The first few hundred million years of the solar system were perilous, as the larger remaining debris was swept away by the new planets' gravity. The fingerprints of this period of heavy bombardment can still be seen in the craters on the Moon, which itself was likely created from Earth in a collision with a large planetesimal, piece of a planet.

The record of that time on Earth has long since been erased by geologic and tectonic processes.

However, the water all around us and the atmosphere we breathe bear witness to the early bombardment that brought ices from the outskirts of the solar nebula to this chunk of rock and metal on which life arose.

The articles compiled for this anthology examine the astronomical factors instrumental in the formation of life on Earth and those that influence its continued success. You will read about the research that scientists are pursuing on a wide range of topics, including where Earth's water came from, when life first appeared and what it looked like, why things turned out different here than on other planets, what the future holds for Earth as the Sun ages, and how likely it is that this whole scenario has occurred elsewhere in our universe. Could we really be alone?

We have no reason to assume Earth is truly unique in harboring life. It orbits an average star, one that is neither too old nor too young, neither too hot nor too cold, at a distance that's neither too close nor too far to support life. Luckily for us, it was, and continues to be, "just right."

But there are aspects of Earth's history whose importance to life we simply can't evaluate yet, since we still only have the life on this planet by which to compare. For example, Earth is unique among the terrestrial planets—those composed of rock and metal and having solid surfaces—in having a giant moon. Some scientists have suggested that the tides that the Moon raises may have helped life gain a foothold in Earth's oceans. In addition, water here might owe its very existence to Jupiter and the gravity it wields in the solar system.

The chemicals for life are all around us in the universe. At what point these chemicals make the transition to life poses one of the most important questions in science today, and one that is extremely hard to answer. All traces of early life-forms on Earth have long since been absorbed into a larger ecosystem. The answer to this crucial question lies in finding complex chemicals in other worlds in the solar system that are just on the verge of "becoming" life and in studying the most primitive organisms that result from this transition.

In 1996, scientists analyzing a meteorite from Mars reported finding fossilized microscopic structures similar in appearance to primitive bacteria on Earth. While the nature of those structures is still unknown, the announcement generated a wave of public interest and marked the debut of a new scientific specialization: astrobiology. Through the Astrobiology Institute, NASA is pursuing three broad questions: How does life begin and evolve? Is there life elsewhere in the universe? And what is the future of life on Earth and beyond?

Answering the first question in particular requires expertise across many sciences. Astronomers, geologists, climatologists, and geophysicists are putting together a history of Earth's formation and early environment. At the same time, chemists, biologists, and paleontologists are piecing together the steps life took on the way from organic molecules to complex organisms. All are working together to compose a coherent picture that describes the rise of life on Earth, one that can be applied to other terrestrial planets as they are found.

Understanding which factors influence whether a planet can harbor life requires finding and studying planets around other stars to gain a clearer picture of how solar systems form. Although all the planets found to date appear to be gas giants—planets such as Jupiter and Saturn, composed mostly of gas, which cannot harbor life as we know it—future space missions like the Terrestrial Planet Finder (TPF) will search for Earth-sized planets and the presence of life. TPF is one of the missions planned by NASA as part of its Origins program, which is dedicated to answering the questions of how and where planets form, what makes them capable of supporting life, and whether extraterrestrial life exists.

This anthology will introduce you to a field that is still in its infancy. As scientists attempt to answer these questions in the coming decades, you can learn with them long after leaving school. These are some of the most profound questions that exist. Though it may be many years before we have answers, we can take comfort in knowing that asking them is what makes us human. —*EM*

1 Radiation from Space

Gamma ray bursts (GRBs) are extremely energetic flares of gamma rays, the most energetic light that exists. GRBs last for less than 100 seconds, though an afterglow detected as X-rays or visible light may last for weeks or months. GRBs are believed to originate in distant galaxies; astronomers suspect that GRBs occur during the creation of black holes, either out of massive stars or massive stellar remnants such as neutron stars.

Either type of creation of black hole could occur in the Milky Way. If a GRB happened nearby, the effect on Earth would be catastrophic. In fact, some scientists have suggested that past mass extinctions uncovered in the fossil record may have been caused by GRBs. A similar global catastrophe with a different astronomical origin arrived with the impact of an asteroid or comet 65 million years ago, at the end of the Cretaceous period. That impact darkened the skies, cooled Earth, and led to the extinction of the dinosaurs.

The details of how a GRB in the Milky Way might affect Earth will give you a sense of how life remains at the mercy of events beyond our control, and Dr. Jerry Bonnell in "A Bad Day in the Milky Way" will help you put it in perspective. —EM

"A Bad Day in the Milky Way"
by Dr. Jerry Bonnell
PBS.org, January 2002

For me, one of the compelling ironies borne of discoveries in astronomy over the past few decades is the contrast between the detection of planets outside our solar system, which has fueled speculations about life beyond Earth, and the discovery of perhaps the most violent, inhospitable events in the universe—gamma-ray bursts—which have fueled speculation about a conceivable end to life on Earth.

Unlike the detection of extrasolar planets, for which astronomers were actively searching, the discovery of gamma-ray bursts—sudden unpredictable flashes of high-energy photons coming from space—was serendipitous. In the 1960s, the U.S. Air Force launched a series of satellites designed to verify the conditions of the Nuclear Test Ban Treaty, whose signatories, including the United States, Britain, and the Soviet Union, agreed not to test nuclear devices in the atmosphere or in space. Called Vela, from the Spanish verb *velar* ("to watch"), the satellites bore experimental detectors intended to give the U.S. a means to monitor nuclear bomb tests. In a 1973 publication, Ray Klebesadel, Ian Strong, and Roy Olson of the Los Alamos Scientific Laboratory announced that Vela gamma-ray detectors had indeed picked up high-energy gamma-ray flashes—but they originated not from Earth but from deep space. Busily scanning Earth for gamma rays from nuclear explosions, Vela satellites inadvertently discovered the most violent celestial explosions since the Big Bang.

Gamma-ray bursts may sound exotic, but they are actually quite common. During the 1990s, the so-called Burst And Transient Source Experiment (BATSE), an instrument aboard NASA's orbiting Compton Gamma Ray Observatory, found that bursts lasting from fractions of a second to tens or hundreds of seconds occurred roughly once a day. In orbit in 1991, nearly 30 years after the first Velas, BATSE ("battsy") was the most sensitive detector of cosmic gamma-ray bursts ever constructed. But even BATSE could only watch the gamma-ray emissions from the bursters fade away, never to be seen again and leaving no clearly identifiable trace of their sources. Nevertheless, BATSE could determine the general direction in which each of the gamma-ray bursts occurred. Early BATSE maps of locations of gamma-ray bursters showed that bursts came not only at random times but from random directions.

Striking Fear

The BATSE results struck fear into the hearts of astrophysicists around the planet. Well, maybe not fear, but some did seem to experience symptoms of "ergophobia" (fear of energy). The concerns arose after it was realized that a startling but natural explanation of the bursters' random positions and observed brightness was that they were located in distant galaxies, themselves randomly distributed in our sky. Now, to be in galaxies far, far away and yet detectable on Earth, the burst sources, whatever they are, had to release truly enormous energies—tremendous but distant explosions only faintly "heard." Instead of a nuclear bomb-sized hiccough from a nearby neutron star, such truly cosmological distances (i.e., in the billions of light-years) to the bursters seemed to require the sudden conversion of a significant fraction of a star with the mass of the sun into gamma rays a la Einstein's famous equation $E = mc^2$. The idea of such extreme energies led many to search for other explanations of the BATSE results.

The cosmological distance scale to at least some of the burst sources is now firmly established, though. The observational breakthrough came in 1997 when BeppoSAX, an Italian/Dutch X-ray astronomy satellite, was able to identify X-ray afterglows of gamma-ray bursts. The fading afterglows were visible long after the gamma-ray burst emission had disappeared, and BeppoSAX located them well enough to permit follow-on observations with large, ground-based optical telescopes. The burst sources were clearly seen to lie in galaxies billions of light-years distant, confirming the enormous energies produced.

In addition to fading afterglows, prompt optical emission was actually detected while a gamma-ray burst was in progress in 1999. This first-ever visible light image of an ongoing gamma-ray burst was recorded by the automated Robotic Optical Transient Search Experiment (ROTSE-I) operating at Los Alamos, home of the original satellite-borne cosmic gamma-ray detectors. Impressively, if that burst had occurred in our own galaxy at a distance of about 3,000 light-years, the direct optical emission would momentarily have appeared to us at least as bright as the noonday sun.

Bursting Earth

In the early 1990s, however, astrophysicists hotly debated the significance of the BATSE results, including the implied distances and energies. This debate led to thoughts of what would happen if a burst occurred in our galactic neighborhood.

Wondering if any other lines of evidence might point toward such extreme postulated energies for gamma-ray bursts, for instance, Princeton University's Steve Thorsett, writing in the May 1995 *Astrophysical Journal Letters*, calculated some terrestrial consequences that might be expected if gamma-ray bursts really were at cosmological distances. He asked, what if such a burst occurred somewhere within our own galaxy, say only thousands of light-years away? Building on past researchers' descriptions of the consequences of a nearby supernova or exploding star, Thorsett outlined in general terms a disheartening scenario of a local gamma-ray burster firing its energetic photons at planet Earth.

Regardless of the mechanism producing the burst, the intense flux of gamma rays would likely be stopped in the lower stratosphere by collisions with atmospheric nitrogen molecules. The molecules would break up and reform as nitric oxide and related compounds. (Hanging over cities today, nitric oxides are the brownish constituents of smog; they are also catalysts for the destruction of ozone.) Uncheerful brown skies and stratospheric ozone destruction would initially affect only the hemisphere facing the gamma-ray burst, but winds would soon spread the destruction worldwide.

How much ozone would be destroyed? Thorsett estimated that if the burster were located near the center of our galaxy, some 30,000 light-years away, the ozone depletion would be a few percent, comparable to that produced by natural disasters like large volcanic eruptions, very intense solar flares, or even a meteor impact on the scale of the one that exploded over Tunguska, Siberia in 1908.

If the burster were closer, say less than 3,000 light-years away, the gamma-ray flux received in a few tens of seconds could wipe out the entire ozone layer for years to come. At the very least, the drastic increase in solar ultraviolet radiation reaching Earth's surface would cause severe skin cancers. For humans and other animals, slow starvation would likely result, as the harmful ultraviolet flux inhibited plant growth and damaged and altered ecosystems supporting the food chain. As in a nuclear winter, the nitric oxides darkening our skies could also cause acid rains and significant cooling of the Earth's surface. Such pollutants would take decades to settle out of the stratosphere.

But that's not all. In addition to the chemical changes in the atmosphere, the nuclear interactions induced by the high-energy gamma rays would rapidly produce huge quantities of radioactive nucleids, such as carbon-14, which has a half-life of 5,700 years. Of course, winds would distribute this fallout worldwide.

It Gets Worse

Depending on what the mechanism for producing a gamma-ray burst actually is, a nearby burst could wreak even more havoc. Nir Shaviv and Arnon Dar of the Israel Institute of Technology have explored a particularly devastating model for generating gamma-ray bursts from co-orbiting pairs of neutron stars. All neutron star pairs eventually spiral together, losing energy through gravitational radiation as predicted by Einstein's theory of general relativity.

Shaviv and Dar postulate that as the neutron stars begin their own catastrophic merger, jets of matter would be flung from the system at nearly the speed of light. These atoms and ions would be so energetic that they would absorb visible starlight and re-emit gamma rays, which we would detect as a gamma-ray burst. Impinging on our fair planet shortly after the horrific flash of gamma rays, the energetic particles themselves would join in the destruction, triggering still more deadly atmospheric cascades of nuclear interactions lasting up to a month.

These authors and others note that known pairs of neutron stars exist in our galaxy, including one within about 1,500 light-years. This knowledge has led to the speculation that in the past the Earth has found itself uncomfortably close to a violent neutron star merger. Some estimates hold that one occurs within about 3,000 light-years of the sun every 100 million years on average. Intriguingly, this timescale is roughly the same as the time between mass extinctions in our planet's geological record.

Learn to Love the Burst

One shouldn't worry too much, though. For one thing, mass extinctions in the past might have been the result of purely terrestrial phenomena, such as climatic changes produced by plate tectonics and volcanic activity, or of more familiar kinds of cosmic disasters, like the asteroid impact thought to have caused the dinosaur extinction at the end of the Cretaceous Period. For another, even if the aforementioned scenarios turned out to be true, we would still have, statistically speaking, about 50 million years until the next gamma-ray burst of doom.

Which gives us time to get to know bursters better. Our understanding of them constantly changes as new findings are reported. For instance, recent afterglow studies have indicated that a burst's energy is beamed in a particular direction rather than radiating in all directions from the source, substantially reducing the burster's total energy requirement.

Moreover, even after three decades of study, the true nature of gamma-ray bursts remains unknown. Many astrophysicists have taken a shine to a new theory, which for the moment has eclipsed the neutron-star-merger

17

scenario in popularity. Evidence is mounting that at least some bursters are more likely associated with star-forming regions than with binary neutron stars. Theoretical models now in vogue indicate that gamma-ray bursts result from "hypernovae"—the collapse of the cores of extremely short-lived massive stars into black holes.

Another theory actually paints gamma-ray bursts in a positive light. University College Dublin researchers Brian McBreen and Lorraine Hanlon recently estimated the effects of a nearby gamma-ray burst on the preplanetary solar nebula, the cloud of condensing star stuff that formed our solar system some 4.5 billion years ago. They calculated that iron in the nebula would have been the major absorber of the high-energy X-rays and gamma rays from such a burst, causing the nebula's dust to become molten in seconds and then cooling slowly to form millimeter-sized chondrules, round granules of cosmic origin. Chondrules, they note, combined to form meteorites and possibly the rocky terrestrial planets, including Earth.

So, you see, despite the gloom-and-doom scenario I painted above, perhaps we should call them bursts of life.

Reprinted with permission from Dr. Jerry Bonnell.

In the wispy, faint corona of the Sun—the outer layer of the Sun visible only during total

solar eclipses—atoms are heated to temperatures reaching millions of degrees and are thus ionized into their component protons and electrons. These charged particles constantly stream away from the Sun in what is called the solar wind, which typically moves outward at speeds of 249 miles per second (400 kilometers per second).

Once these particles reach Earth, they encounter the "protective bubble" of Earth's magnetosphere, the magnetic lines of force that originate in Earth's liquid core and reach out far beyond its atmosphere. Because the particles are charged, they interact with the magnetosphere. The magnetosphere traps the particles of the solar wind and keeps them from reaching Earth's surface, where they would be harmful to life.

Solar wind particles typically spiral along Earth's magnetic field high above the poles, resulting in the displays of light known as aurora borealis and aurora australis, or the northern and southern lights. Occasionally, though, the magnetosphere experiences violent "substorms" that produce shimmering and colorful auroras, but which have also damaged satellites and power grids.

The goal of the mission called Time History of Events and Macroscopic Interactions During Substorms (THEMIS) is to find

the cause of these substorms and provide a
better understanding of the magnetosphere
that shields us. —EM

"Into the Sphere of Fire"
by Stephen Battersby
New Scientist, **August 2, 2003**

There are three realms of the Earth that we know well: the sphere of rock, the sphere of water and the sphere of air. But there is a fourth realm that is almost unknown. A hundred thousand kilometres into space, the Earth's magnetic field traps ionised gases at temperatures of more than 10 million degrees. This realm of fire, called the magnetosphere, protects us from cosmic radiation. But it is an unsteady shield.

The magnetosphere is occasionally rocked by an explosive convulsion that flings some of its energies at the Earth, switching on spectacular auroras, damaging satellites, and knocking out electric power grids. No one knows what triggers these violent events, but now an expedition is being put together to find out. THEMIS, a flotilla of five spacecraft, has been given the go-ahead by NASA to enter the sphere of fire and discover what makes it so unstable. THEMIS should tell us what is behind the dancing lights of the aurora, and solve the mystery of how our cosmic protector works.

The magnetosphere is a kind of elastic fire. It forms where the Earth's magnetic field meets the hot plasma ionised gases at the edge of the planet's atmosphere.

The magnetic field exerts a force on the electrically charged particles within the plasma, and as they move within the field, they in turn generate their own magnetic field. The net result is that the field and the plasma become "glued" together into a single substance that is threaded by strong electric currents: one flows sideways across the tail, for example, and a "ring current" in the inner magnetosphere circles the Earth.

Left to itself, the magnetosphere would be as spherical as its name suggests. However, the solar wind, a stream of particles emanating from the sun, pulls the outer layer of this elastic fire along with it like wind-blown hair. So, while the inner part remains spherical, the outer part is distorted into a comet-like shape, with a round head about 10 times the planet's diameter on the side facing the sun, and a long tail stretched out on the opposite side, away from the sun.

The frequent convulsions that shake up this settled arrangement are caused by the solar wind's magnetic field. It is extremely weak at only a few nanoteslas, it is about a millionth of the field generated by a typical fridge magnet but the chaotic flow of the solar wind means that this field is constantly shifting around. Much of the time it lines up with Earth's field, and simply flows around the Earth like a stream flowing around a boulder. But when the magnetic field turns, so that it runs contrary to the Earth's field, things get nasty.

As the opposing fields are pushed together, they can join up in a process called magnetic reconnection. This reconfigured field peels off and moves around to the tail, intensifying the field behind the Earth. This can't go on for ever; eventually something snaps, and then all hell breaks loose. Giant gobbets of plasma are hurled at high speed along the tail. A powerful electric current that normally flows across the tail instead cascades down to Earth, and 100 kilometres above the Earth's surface the writhing curtains of the aurora flare up and migrate towards the poles.

"These phenomena happen within a couple of minutes, like an explosion of energy," says Vassilis Angelopoulos of the Space Sciences Laboratory at the University of California, Berkeley. They take place so fast, in fact, that no one has yet been able to work out for sure what kicks the whole thing off.

According to one theory, the trigger is in the tail. In the core of the tail two magnetic fields point in opposite directions: one is heading outwards from the Earth's south pole; the other runs inwards towards the north pole. As the tail is squeezed and elongated by the solar wind, its field stores energy like a stretched piece of elastic. Eventually, the tail snaps: in a small region around 25 Earth radii (Re) out, the opposing fields on opposite sides of the tail link up and the magnetic tension is suddenly released. This catapults one blob of plasma down the tail away from us, and another earthwards. Each plasma bullet is bigger than our planet and hotter than the sun.

Fortunately, the one heading our way doesn't get to ground level unimpeded. "At about 8 to 10 Re it piles up against the rigid magnetic field of the inner

22

magnetosphere," says Robert McPherron of the University of California, Los Angeles. This impact disrupts the electric current flowing across the tail, he thinks, diverting some of it to flow parallel to the magnetic field, towards the Earth. The energetic electrons that form the current hit molecules of the outer atmosphere, making them glow and so creating the aurora.

Although most of this sequence of events is uncontroversial, many physicists don't think that magnetic reconnection is the trigger. Anthony Lui of Johns Hopkins University in Baltimore, Maryland, is one of them. He believes that the plasma and magnetic field are glued together so tightly that reconnection is not likely to happen spontaneously: something else has to break that glue. Lui believes it all begins with the current in the magnetosphere's tail.

Whereas the plasma as a whole is glued to the magnetic field, individual electrons and ions can spiral around magnetic field lines. The diameter of the spiral depends on the energy and mass of each particle: ions travel in much fatter spirals than electrons, and go in the opposite direction. Throughout most of the magnetosphere these gyrations cancel out, so there is no net movement of charge. But right in the middle of the tail, at the point where the direction of the magnetic field switches over, the motions of charges don't cancel, and that leaves a net electric current.

When the solar wind pushes some magnetic field from the head round to the tail, the resulting compression of the tail makes the magnetic discontinuity at its core sharper, and so increases the cross-tail current. And currents flowing inside plasmas are notoriously unstable. Eventually, Lui thinks, the current becomes too strong to be stable and starts to thrash around like a loose garden hose. Some of this loose current arcs down to Earth to generate the aurora, while waves of turbulence generated by this instability spread out along the tail. This breaks the glue that normally maintains the tail's twin magnetic fields, and allows them to reconnect.

Judgement Day

In principle it should be simple to tell which theory is right. If current disruption is the root cause of these "substorms," it will happen first and be followed by reconnection; if reconnection is the trigger it will happen first and be followed by a change in the flow of current. The obvious way to decide is to station sentries at the crucial points in the magnetosphere to time exactly when these events take place and that is exactly what THEMIS is designed to do.

The name stands for "time history of events and macroscale interactions during substorms." Themis is also the ancient Greek goddess of impartial justice, and the hope is that she will provide the necessary objectivity to put an end to the 30 years of heated arguments about the true trigger of magnetic substorms.

According to the THEMIS team, four satellites ought to be enough to do the job, but they are playing safe and launching five. The spare craft will act as a back-up in case one fails. If all goes well, three craft will pass through the region where the cross-tail current is disrupted. The fourth will go about twice as far away, looping out to 20 Re, while the fifth will go way out to 30 Re, which is about halfway to the moon. These outer two will straddle the region where the magnetic field in the tail is thought to reconnect.

Each probe will carry an array of detectors for measuring electric and magnetic fields, and the trajectories and energies of electrons and ions in the plasma. This information should reveal when something violent is happening nearby: the magnetic field will jump around, and there will be a sudden jump in the number of high-energy particles hitting the spacecraft.

The crucial thing is to be in the right place at the right time. The five orbits have been chosen so that every four days all the spacecraft come into conjunction in a long line stretching outwards along the magnetosphere's tail. The inner three craft will have orbits with a period of exactly one day, the fourth will orbit in two days, and the fifth in four days. When they are aligned, they should be ideally placed to fix the time and the place of the key stages of a substorm, telling us whether reconnection or current disruption happens first.

In addition to the spacecraft and the tracking stations needed to receive and process data, there will be a network of more than 50 ground stations, mostly in Canada and Alaska, that will time the onset of auroral displays. Taken together, this will tell THEMIS researchers about the relative timing of the reconnection, current disruption and the brightening and expansion of the auroral emissions that define a substorm.

The whole project comes with a modest price tag of $160 million, far less than many single space probes. "Many people still don't believe we can do it," says Angelopoulos, the mission's lead scientist. If all goes to plan, THEMIS should launch in 2007. Angelopoulos calculates that in the first year of operation, it should catch some 35 substorms in the act and solve the mystery of reconnections.

Apart from its interest to physicists, will the data THEMIS gathers be of any practical use? Angelopoulos is confident it will help us predict the onset of severe space weather caused by a series of substorms. But far more destructive than substorms are the full-blown magnetic storms that occur when a particularly fast or dense stream in the solar wind hits Earth. The crucial sign of a storm is that the ring current circling the Earth becomes much stronger. Acting like an electromagnet, this current can generate a magnetic field in opposition to Earth's. This weakens the protection provided by the magnetosphere, exposing satellites and astronauts to intense radiation from space. In 1994, for example, two Canadian communications satellites, Anik E-1 and Anik E-2, failed. Electrical charges are thought to have built up within them during a storm, causing damage to their circuitry when they discharged. One of the satellites was out of control for months.

The enhanced ring current may also induce currents on the Earth's surface that can overload electrical power grids. In 1989, for instance, such an event brought down Quebec's entire power supply system. Six million people were cut off for 9 hours, and the cost ran into hundreds of millions of dollars.

The best hope of avoiding such disasters is to predict them, but before we can do that we need to understand their cause. Some researchers think that substorms can stack up to create full-blown storms. Since substorms inject power into the ring current, it perhaps seems natural to suppose that a rapid sequence of violent substorms could contribute to a storm. "Most strong storms are associated with intense substorms," says Lui. "There are a few storms without substorms," he admits, "but these are usually weaker ones."

Others insist that storms are entirely separate phenomena. McPherron, for instance, says that in a storm, the magnetic field of the solar wind can peel and push Earth's field in a continuous motion and that this is wholly responsible for boosting the ring current. Substorms, he says, are irrelevant.

THEMIS should resolve this issue, too. If it catches a series of substorms occurring during a storm, its instruments should be able to show whether they are powerful enough to be causing the storm, or are just squalls on the surface of a larger weather pattern. And getting a picture of how storms develop should make it easier to predict whether a building storm is going to wreak havoc.

At present, our knowledge of the sphere of fire amounts to little more than a dead map of the magnetosphere, because we lack a real grasp of how this protective shield moves and works. THEMIS will bring the picture to life. And as well as showing us what causes auroras on Earth, it will also indicate how they form elsewhere. The magnetospheres of Mercury and Jupiter probably behave in the same way as Earth's, as would any magnetic field buffeted by a magnetic wind on any planet in the universe. So when THEMIS pronounces judgement, we will understand what drives the dancing lights on countless alien worlds.

Reprinted with permission from *New Scientist.*

While all the planets lie in roughly the same plane of the solar system, each planet's orbit has its own slight tilt. Even if all the planets are on the same side of the Sun, each is a different distance above or below the plane. Perfect alignments of any planets as seen from Earth, therefore, happen only rarely. In any case, the direct gravitational effect such alignments have on Earth is negligible since gravity decreases rapidly with increasing distance. But solar systems are complicated, and it is impossible to measure the movement of so many bodies accurately enough to predict their future orbits.

In physics, a "chaotic" system is one in which slight changes in initial conditions lead to unpredictable behavior in the long term. Astronomers have found that planetary orbits are chaotic, needing only small changes to make them unpredictable. Chaos in Saturn's orbit, as described in this article, could result

*in its more frequent alignments with Jupiter.
Their combined gravitational forces would
spread chaos to the orbits of nearby asteroids,
and that really could have disastrous consequences for life on Earth. Exactly such a
period of chaos may have sent an asteroid
into Earth some 65 million years ago and the
dinosaurs into extinction. —EM*

"Chaotic Heavens"
by Marcus Chown
New Scientist, February 28, 2004

It was Isaac Newton who finally showed why the
heavenly bodies move in predictable ways. He proved
that the planets move in response to the sun's gravitational pull, endlessly repeating their orbits like
celestial clockwork. If you know the position and
velocity of a planet today, you can work out its motion
far into the future.

Or so we thought until recently. "Our research
shows that for tens of millions of years, the planets
orbit the sun with the regularity of clockwork," says
geophysicist Michael Ghil. "Then, quite unexpectedly,
everything goes crazy." According to Ghil, who works
at the Ecole Normale Superieure in Paris and the
University of California at Los Angeles, this planetary
madness is all down to chaos. In chaotic systems, tiny
changes in conditions can lead to huge differences in
outcome. Though you can predict what the changes will

do in theory, the system is so sensitive that you'll never get it right.

If the only consequence was a little unpredictability, that would perhaps be a shame, but not too troubling—just a slight departure from Newton's clockwork ideal. But it's much worse than that. According to Ghil's latest work, carried out with Ferenc Varadi and Bruce Runnegar at UCLA, the solar system's chaotic nature can also unleash an asteroid storm, flinging massive rocks out of their usual orbits and showering the solar system's inner planets with debris. It may even have been what killed the dinosaurs.

We have known for a while now that the planets aren't as stable as we like to think. If the Earth and sun were alone in space, Earth would trace out an elliptical or circular orbit. In the case of this "two-body" system, the path can be predicted exactly. But the solar system is more complicated. In addition to the steady gravitational pull of the sun, each planet feels smaller, varying tugs from the other eight planets and all the various moons. Mathematicians have proved that it is impossible to solve Newton's equations exactly even when there are as few as three bodies present, let alone dozens. Instead, scientists have to make approximations about a planet's position and the forces it experiences, and these errors can grow over time and send orbital calculations wildly off beam.

In 1988 Gerry Sussman at MIT, working with Jack Wisdom at the University of California, Santa Barbara, worked out that Pluto's orbit is chaotic. In other words, if you try to predict the shape of Pluto's elliptical orbit around the sun in the long term, your calculation will be extremely sensitive to the parameters you put in at the start. A year later, Wisdom and Jacques Laskar of the Bureau des Longitudes in Paris proved that the Earth's orbit is also chaotic. They showed that an error as small as 15 metres in measuring the position of the Earth today would make it impossible to predict where the planet will be in its orbit in 100 million years' time.

But Ghil and his colleagues have also discovered a more disturbing way that chaos can creep in. They were wondering what influence Jupiter and Saturn might have, and suspected that when the two biggest planets in the solar system line up in front of the sun, in the same way that the Earth, moon and sun align during a total solar eclipse, their gravitational pull could cause dramatic effects. Under the right conditions, they thought, these gas giants might be able to nudge a nearby celestial body into a more elongated orbit.

Like solar eclipses, this alignment between Jupiter, Saturn and the sun is rare. In the time it takes Saturn to complete two orbits around the sun, Jupiter has whizzed round almost five times. This means that the planets are only on the same side of the sun as each other every 20 years.

But that's not the end of the story. The orbit Saturn makes around the sun lies in a slightly different plane to Jupiter's orbit. In other words, the planets' pathways are inclined to each other. So every 20 years when

Jupiter overtakes Saturn, the planets do not line up exactly: Saturn usually lies above or below Jupiter. This means that the combined gravitational pull of the two gas giants is much weaker than it would be if the planets were in perfect alignment.

If Jupiter made precisely five orbits for every two that Saturn makes, the planets would never line up with each other perfectly. But because the ratio is not exactly 5:2, the point where they pass slowly moves round the sun. As the planets get closer to perfect alignment, the extra tug they exert on other planets, moons and asteroids becomes stronger. The gravitational pull is strongest when Jupiter eventually overtakes Saturn at precisely the point where the orbits cross each other. "The effect on other bodies in the solar system rises to a crescendo every 1,000 or so years," says Ghil.

Until now, most planetary scientists have ignored this occasional extra pull from Jupiter and Saturn in their models of the solar system because it happens so infrequently. Over long periods of time, they reasoned, this additional tug would be of little consequence.

"We weren't sure this was right," says Ghil. And so his group set out to study its effects in detail. To do that, they had to follow in the footsteps of 18th-century astronomers and construct an orrery, a machine that displays how the planets move relative to one another. But this would be no mechanical orrery. While early astronomers used cogs and wheels, modern planetary scientists use digital orreries, computer models dedicated to simulating complex planetary motions.

Although they still use approximations in their computations, Ghil, Varadi and Runnegar have constructed the most accurate digital orrery ever built. It crunches the numbers on finer time intervals than any other, thereby revealing much greater detail. With this, they can start with the positions of the planets and asteroids today and wind back the clock to see how the solar system looked tens of millions of years ago (*Icarus*, vol 139, p 286).

What the team found is remarkable. Jupiter and Saturn's orbits are poised on a knife-edge: most of the time their orbits are pretty much predictable, but the slightest disturbance can send them into chaos—meaning they become beset by unpredictable variations. Because such systems are so complex, it is impossible to pinpoint which aspect of a planet's orbit might go haywire. "The chaos might, for instance, manifest itself in wild variations in the length of Jupiter's orbit, its inclination or even its orientation," says Ghil.

Working out what could tip Jupiter and Saturn into chaotic orbits is a mammoth task, so Ghil's team focused on just one factor. They reasoned that, over hundreds of millions of years, non-gravitational effects such as the pressure of sunlight and particles in the solar wind, could have affected Saturn's orbit. The team wound the clock back millions of years to a time when the planet's furthest point from the sun—a parameter called the semi-major axis—was 0.1 per cent

less than now. "We think such a change is entirely plausible," says Ghil.

His team found that this perturbation disrupts Saturn's orbit to the point where it becomes wobbly and "aperiodic"—each revolution around the sun takes a slightly different path from the last one. This means that, at certain times, the orbits of Saturn and Jupiter might be in virtually the same plane producing a much stronger gravitational pull than usual. This has the potential to unleash havoc in the solar system. In particular, it can trigger chaotic instability in the asteroid belt that lies between the orbits of Mars and Jupiter. "I can certainly believe that changing Saturn's semi-major axis under certain conditions may lead to an instability in the planetary system," says Alessandro Morbidelli, a mathematician working on chaotic dynamics in the solar system at the Cote d'Azur Observatory in Nice, France.

It's all down to the way the planets can transfer their energy to nearby objects with particular orbits. In the same way as you can make a child's swing go higher if you push it at the right moment, Jupiter and Saturn can push asteroids from a regular orbit into a chaotic one. In the case of the child's swing, you transfer energy most efficiently if you shove the swing at a frequency known as the resonant frequency. Similarly, Jupiter and Saturn have more of an effect on asteroids whose orbital frequency around the sun forms an integer ratio with one of their orbital frequencies. For instance, an asteroid that goes round the sun three times for every two turns by Jupiter is said to be in a 3:2 resonance. And if an asteroid is in a resonant orbit, chaos in Jupiter's orbit can trigger a large and unpredictable change in the asteroid's path.

As yet, says Ghil, it is impossible to tell how long the chaotic effect on the asteroid belt persists, but they have calculated the likely outcome. "We find an incredible wealth of effects," he says. Some asteroids swing from their usual orbits into ones that are closer to the sun, while others fly out to larger, elongated orbits. "A whole population of asteroids can drift back and forth through a succession of resonant orbits," says Ghil.

Most of these asteroids stay within the asteroid belt, but crucially, Ghil has found that the gravitational pull of other planets can yank some rocky bodies free of the asteroid belt altogether. "Some are even catapulted into orbits that cross the Earth's," he says.

This is exactly what Ghil and his colleagues' digital orrery says happened 65 million years ago. As if some mischievous god had reached in and stirred things up, the solar system suddenly became a hornets' nest of activity. Chaos in the Jupiter-Saturn system caused a flurry of Earth-crossing asteroids, and among them may have been the one thought to have had the dinosaurs' name written on it. Something certainly crashed off the Yucatan coast in Mexico at the end of the Cretaceous period, just when the dinosaurs died out. "We can't say we've actually caught the culprit that fell into the Yucatan peninsula yet but we're on its trail," says Ghil. "The dinosaurs might have been the victims of an event hard-wired into the dynamics of the solar system."

Ghil and his colleagues first suggested a link between chaos and the Cretaceous-Tertiary boundary in 2001. Since then, their digital orrery has been working hard to refine the calculations, and they are now confident that the last burst of chaos in the skies did indeed occur at that significant point 65 million years ago (*Astrophysical Journal*, vol 592 p 620).

And last year, Ghil's team calculated that another burst of planetary chaos occurred about 250 million years ago, give or take 10 million years. They speculate that it may be linked to the catastrophic impact event that many believe was responsible for wiping out 95 per cent of species at the end of the Permian period, 251 million years ago. Ghil is not worried about the 10 million year uncertainty. He points out that simulating the solar system with his digital orrery becomes difficult beyond 70 million years. As you look further back in time, the accuracy of the calculations deteriorates due to uncertainties in the current position of the planets. The timing of this burst of chaos is at the very limit of the digital orrery's precision, so it may be possible to link it with the Permian-Triassic boundary.

Such suggestions are contentious, of course. Indeed, not all palaeontologists are convinced that the mass extinction at the end of the Permian was due to an asteroid impact. Many believe that a massive and prolonged volcanic eruption may have been the real culprit.

Finding evidence to corroborate the chaos theory will be difficult. Some of the asteroids stirred up at this time will have been flung into orbits crossing Mars and Venus, so other planets and moons should be scarred with 65 million-year-old impact craters. But strong winds and other weather effects erode ancient craters on planets, making them difficult to date. And although our moon has no atmosphere to weather its craters, past geological activity makes it extremely difficult to date impacts accurately.

But whatever the truth about the dinosaurs, we are still gaining a new understanding of Newton's "clockwork" heavens. Ghil's work is one of several watershed discoveries that is changing our view of the solar system, says Thomas Quinn at the University of Washington in Seattle. Though our solar system evolves quietly and sensibly for tens of millions of years, it also goes through periods of madness, and what has happened in the distant past will happen again. "Our simulations last year show that another burst of chaos is due in 30 million years time," says Ghil.

Should we be worried? Well, when the dinosaurs met their untimely end, seemingly insignificant animals ended up inheriting the Earth. Look around you today. Our successors may already be waiting in the wings.

Reprinted with permission from *New Scientist*.

Astronomers are still uncertain about the details of how the planets formed. The general picture for more than 100 years has been that the process started gently, with bits of dust condensing out of the solar nebula and coming together like snowflakes on a snowball to form planetesimals. Planetesimals are pieces of planets. These planetesimals then began to collide. By colliding, these pieces of planets came to be the mature planets we see today.

However, questions still remain. One of them concerns the existence of chondrules—spheres of silicate rock and metals between 0.5 and 2 millimeters in diameter—found inside meteorites and thought by some scientists to have been the basis for the coalescing planets. Chondrules look like they were initially melted, a puzzling discovery given how cold it is in the asteroid belt from which most meteors come.

Astrophysicist Frank Shu was led by his work on energetic young stars to a theory in which chondrules formed in an intense wind, the "X-wind" blowing from the young Sun. In the theory, the X-wind was hot enough to melt rocky dust and strong enough to carry it outward into the solar system. Shu's theory and its implication for the early solar system are described in this article, "Earth, Wind and Fire," by Hazel Muir. —EM

"Earth, Wind and Fire"
by Hazel Muir
New Scientist, May 17, 2003

In the basement of London's Natural History Museum sit some rocks so ancient they make the demise of the dinosaurs upstairs seem like it was only yesterday. One is from a meteorite that in 1857 made villagers jump out of their skins when it fell to Earth in India, heralded by a fanfare of sonic booms.

Weighing over 70 kilograms and peppered throughout with small round pieces of silicate, the Parnallee meteorite is now giving scientists cause for concern. An analysis suggests that this 4.6 billion-year-old space rock and others like it may be testimony to a dramatic new view of how planets and asteroids formed. Forget tranquil evolution, the Earth may owe its very existence to furious winds that blew red-hot rock out from the Sun at hundreds of kilometres per second.

It's a controversial idea. Until recently all scientists believed that the formation of the Solar System was a fairly sedate affair. For the past two centuries researchers thought asteroids and planets grew from dust and gas that quietly clumped together in a disc of matter orbiting the young Sun. But astrophysicist Frank Shu of the National Tsing Hua University in Hsinchu, Taiwan, now has serious doubts. Analysis of the oldest meteorites has convinced him that the Solar System's youth was much more violent than anyone ever imagined.

Shu hadn't been planning to upset the status quo. He was trying to explain how some embryonic stars blast out energetic streams of hydrogen from their poles. First spotted in the early 1980s, these "bipolar outflows" mystified theorists. Stars are born when a giant cloud of dust and gas collapses to form a spinning star surrounded by a swirling disc of matter. To understand how the torrents of hydrogen form in these young stars, Shu, who was then at the University of California in Berkeley, calculated how the material in the disc interacts with the young star's magnetic field.

According to his model, the burning star heats dust and gas at the inner edge of the disc so fiercely, that electrons are ripped out of the atoms to leave charged ions. Under the influence of the star's magnetic field and gravity, this ionised material falls onto the star. Shu also worked out that all the dust and gas has huge angular momentum, much greater than that of the star itself. According to a key law of physics, the total angular momentum of a closed system must remain the same. Because of this, as the ionised material is sucked inwards, some of it is flung back out at high speed.

Eureka Moment

But Shu's calculations showed something else. The powerful stream of charged particles has a magnetic field of its own, strong enough to change the Sun's field around the dusty disc. Instead of threading through the disc, the magnetic field lines at this point are pinched into an X shape at its inner edge. It was a crucial difference. As gas and dust gravitated in from the cool outer reaches of the disc towards the fiery inner edge, the intense magnetic field here blew them far and wide. Shu called this the X-wind.

He and his colleagues continued to work on the model and found that it could explain the bipolar outflows from embryonic stars that astronomers were seeing with telescopes. But as time passed, he discovered that the X-wind has other talents.

The eureka moment came in the mid-1990s when Shu was in Wellesley, Massachusetts, at a conference on star formation. Al Cameron of the University of Arizona gave a talk on meteorites that have journeyed to Earth from the asteroid belt. He speculated that some kind of wind might explain why most meteorites contain puzzling round blobs of silicates called chondrules, all about a millimetre across. Rich in magnesium and iron, chondrules are thought to have clumped together to produce boulders that went on to attract and merge with other boulders, eventually forming rocky planets in the inner Solar System, including Earth.

The trouble is no one knows how chondrules formed in the first place. They must have started out as loose balls of dust in the cloud of matter surrounding the Sun. But their round shape suggests the dust grains then melted briefly to make a single blob of rock. Scientists suspect that chondrules must have been molten for at least ten minutes. Anything less would have prevented the silicate crystals seen inside chondrules from growing. And if they had been molten for more than an hour, the potassium and sodium they contain would have fizzled out of the globules.

But why did they melt? Most meteorites come from the asteroid belt, which lies between the orbits of Mars and Jupiter. It is a freezing cold place today and it probably wasn't much warmer billions of years ago. "Within the asteroid belt, the temperature was maybe 200 kelvin—that's hardly enough to melt rock," says Shu.

Baffled, physicists had suggested that shock waves in the disc of gas and dust surrounding the Sun could have heated pockets to the temperatures needed to melt the chondrules. Or maybe primeval lightning bolts—electrical discharges in the swirling disc—could have done the trick. "It's always been a mystery how materials in the Solar System were originally heated—after all these years it's frustrating that we still don't know," says Sara Russell, a meteorite expert at the Natural History Museum in London.

Cameron also questioned why chondrules are all about a millimetre across. Very few are twice that size, or half that size. "It's completely unlike what you'd find in a truckload of gravel, for example, where you'd typically see all different sizes from small particles to big particles," says Shu. "The chondrules seem to be size-sorted, just like a can of peas."

At the conference, Cameron argued that if some kind of wind had blown chondrules across the Solar

System, the lightest ones would have drifted farthest while the heavy ones would have been left behind. So the chondrules carried to the narrow asteroid belt—where they could gang together into asteroids and remain in stable orbits—would all, naturally, be roughly the same size.

Shu suddenly realised he had just the kind of wind Cameron was describing—the X-wind. It all fitted together like a jigsaw. "Near the Sun, it's natural to get the temperatures and timescales to melt the chondrules," says Shu. "We know that flares go up in young stars, and they have timescales of an hour. It's natural to think these energetic events can melt rock." And when he went back to his office to do some calculations, he found that the numbers tallied: the X-wind should carry millimetre-sized chondrules from near the Sun to roughly the distance of the asteroid belt.

Although geological changes on the restless Earth have gradually obliterated all traces of the chondrules that originally made up the bulk of our planet, meteorites may still hold plenty of evidence for the X-wind. And when Shu learned that chondrules behave like little bar magnets, it was a further boost for his theory. In fact their magnetisation is so strong, it suggests that the molten droplets of rock solidified in powerful magnetic fields, around 0.1 to 1 millitesla. That's much stronger than the magnetic field on the surface of the Earth (around 0.045 millitesla), let alone way out in the asteroid belt. What these meteorites have recorded, says Shu, is the ancient magnetic field of the Sun near the region where the X-wind launched the chondrules into space.

Things seemed to be going well for the X-wind theory. It could explain a host of strange properties of chondrules and star formation. But it didn't work when Shu and his colleagues tried to use it to explain why certain meteorites contain the remains of a puzzling mix of radioactive elements. So most scientists held on to the traditional view that the radioisotopes were made when a nearby star exploded and got mixed into large globules called calcium-aluminium inclusions (CAIs), which also melted and solidified a long time ago.

It was a tough time for the X-wind theory, but in the past couple of years new data has revived its fortunes. In 2001, Alexander Krot of the University of Hawaii together with Russell at the Natural History Museum and their colleagues reported their conclusions after analysing chondrules in two metal-rich meteorites from Libya and Antarctica. Their analysis suggested the chondrules formed at a temperature of 1,500 kelvin or more, so that moderately volatile elements like sulphur fizzled out of them. But then something must have whipped the chondrules out of the resulting cloud of sulphur vapour, because little sulphur condensed onto them when they cooled (*Science*, vol 291, p 1776). "One way you can do that is if they're suddenly flung outwards in the X-wind," says Russell.

Meanwhile, geochemist Kevin McKeegan of the University of California at Los Angeles and his team found that the famous Allende meteorite that fell onto Mexico in 1969 had once contained radioactive beryllium-10. This was dramatic news because stars never manufacture beryllium-10 in their interiors. Had it instead come from intense radiation processes in the early Solar System, namely the X-wind?

The case in favour of the X-wind strengthened when McKeegan's team found that Allende also once contained beryllium-7. It too is radioactive, but its activity is short-lived with a half-life of only 53 days. So any formed during the birth of the Solar System will have long since vanished, leaving only a characteristic trail of decay products behind.

In Shu's view, the only way Allende's beryllium-7 could come from a supernova—the alternative theory for the formation of radioisotopes in meteorites—would be if the Solar System formed in less than 53 days. Much longer and all the element would have decayed before it could become incorporated into molten globs of rock. "Now no one believes that," he laughs. "The bible talks about seven days, but we think that's metaphorical." For him, the beryllium-7 data is the best clue yet that his X-wind blew out of the young Sun.

Not everyone is convinced. In March, at the Lunar and Planetary Science Conference in Texas, Steven Desch of the Carnegie Institution of Washington argued that galactic cosmic rays could have included heavy

beryllium-10 ions that became trapped in CAIs. And Russell says the beryllium-7 data is controversial, and very difficult to interpret.

Grossman is sceptical that a wind could melt chondrules and CAIs near the Sun, then hurl them all the way out to the asteroid belt to make rocks that "magically" still have the same relative abundances of non-volatile elements as the Sun. More likely, he says, some ingredients would separate out in the wind. He does not worry about the precise size distribution of chondrules. And to him, the X-wind theory is like a chameleon that changes colour every time new data appears. "You've got to watch these theoreticians," says Grossman. "It seems that each time I read a paper about the X-wind, it changes a little."

Other critics are adamant that you simply don't need an X-wind to explain the radioisotopes in CAIs. But most are keeping an open mind. "People have very strong opinions, but I really don't think there's any smoking-gun evidence either way," Russell concludes. She is convinced that clinching evidence will come in the next couple of years, however, when meteorites at the Natural History Museum are probed in greater detail. With Matthieu Gounelle at the University of Paris, she is pioneering measurements of a rare isotope, vanadium-50, in CAIs. The X-wind model predicts they should contain an excess of the isotope vanadium-50, which is stable and so leaves an indelible signature. "That would certainly convince me," says Russell.

More clues about the X-wind will come when spacecraft return samples from asteroids and comets in the next few years. Shu predicts that comets will contain mini chondrules—the ones that the X-wind blew out way beyond Neptune. "Just like a garden sprinkler, the X-wind doesn't just sprinkle chondrules to the asteroid belt, it sprinkles them all over the Solar System," he says.

If he is right, planetary scientists will have to rethink their ideas about how Earth, Mars, Venus and Mercury formed. And it could be grim news for astronomers looking for cosy Earth-like planets around other stars. So far researchers have found more than 100 extrasolar planets, all of them gas giants like Jupiter or Saturn, which planet-hunting techniques find most easily. New projects in the pipeline hope to nail small, rocky, Earth-like planets orbiting their stars in warm zones where liquid water could flow and life could evolve. But if the X-wind theory is right, rocky planets as we know them might be rare.

Chondrules were the seeds for the growth of the rocky planets in our own Solar System, so the Earth may owe its existence to an X-wind that happened to blow just right. Too gentle a breeze wouldn't have returned enough chondrules to the disc of the solar nebula for rocky planets to have formed. Had it blown too hard, the chondrules might have flown far into the frigid realms of the comets. Near other stars, the bricks and mortar for building Earth-like planets may, quite literally, have gone with the wind.

Reprinted with permission from *New Scientist*.

At the time of this writing, astronomers had discovered 136 "exoplanets"—planets orbiting stars other than the Sun. Astronomers search for planets indirectly by looking for the planets' gravitational influence on the stars they orbit. By measuring the planets' gravitational tugs, astronomers have calculated that most of the planets found so far are at least as massive as Jupiter. Most likely, they are also gas giants, incapable of supporting life.

Recently, more sensitive instruments have led to the discovery of planets with masses comparable to Uranus or Neptune, which are still fifteen to seventeen times the mass of Earth. NASA's Terrestrial Planet Finder, currently under development for launch sometime around 2015, has as its primary mission the discovery of Earth-sized planets and the search for signatures of life.

Where might such planets be found? Scientists are now evaluating locations in the galaxy where solar systems are most likely to form. Based on the planets found so far, there is a connection between the amount of "metals" a star has (to an astronomer, any atom heavier than helium is a metal) and the likelihood that

*it will form planets. The results of such research
may eventually be used to target stars for
planet searches. —EM*

"No Place Like Zone"
by Mark A. Garlick
Astronomy, August 2002

Earth has been referred to as the "Goldilocks planet" because its distance from the sun is just right—it's not too hot, and it's not too cold, allowing for life-enabling liquid water to flow freely on our planet's surface. Some astronomers go even further to view Earth's position within the Milky Way Galaxy as an extension of this Goldilocks character. For if it weren't for such fortuitous galactic placement, what scientists have referred to as the galactic habitable zone (GHZ), Earth may well have been scorched by gamma-ray jets, blown away by stellar winds, blasted apart by supernovae explosions, or bombarded by countless comets and asteroids long ago.

In less than a decade, researchers have found nearly 80 planets orbiting just a handful of stars—all of which lie in the sun's neighborhood. These results have been cheered right across the astronomical community. For if such a relatively tiny region of space is rife with planets, this raises the probability that exoplanets are common throughout the galaxy, even across the universe. From there, it's just a baby step to believing that life might be common too. But if new research into the characteristics of the GHZ is correct, then terrestrial life-bearing exoplanets—if they exist—will not be distributed randomly across the Milky Way. These earthlike worlds will be limited to within a narrow annulus centered on the galactic core and containing the sun. Outside of this zone, some astronomers now contend, the Milky Way might be as sterile as the surface of the moon.

Getting to the Zone

The GHZ is a relatively new idea, as we shall see. But the concept of the Circumstellar Habitable Zone (CHZ), often abbreviated to just "habitable zone," first appeared in the scientific literature in the 1950s. Very simply, the habitable zone is defined as that region around a star where water—regarded by many as essential for life—exists in liquid form on the surface of a planet long enough to nurture the evolution of life. If the planet is too close to the star, water will evaporate and the planet overheats. If it's too far out, water freezes. The zone's definition varies from time to time and may not contain strictly all possible life-bearing worlds. For example, the jovian moon Europa is well outside the sun's habitable zone and yet is regarded by many scientists as one of the two most likely places in the solar system (the other being Mars) where extraterrestrial life might exist. The CHZ has its merits, and since the 1980s various researchers have considered extensions to this concept on the galactic scale.

For example, some believe that the sun's place-ment near the so-called co-rotation radius aided the development of complex life on Earth. The co-rotation radius is the distance from the galactic core where the orbital period of the sun around the core matches the rotation timescale of the galaxy's spiral arms. The spi-ral arms do not revolve at the same speed as the stars themselves, except near the co-rotation radius. Because the sun is so close to the co-rotation circle, this minimizes the number of times the sun crosses a spiral arm, thereby avoiding the infusion of a super-dense stellar environment. This is important because perturbations from nearby stars could send some of the Oort Cloud's many cometary nuclei spiraling into the inner solar system to wreak havoc on Earth. If those perturbations come too regularly, as they would if the sun were far outside the co-rotation radius and crossed the denser spiral arms more often, then the development of life on Earth would have likely faced a fierce uphill battle.

But protection within the realm of the co-rotation radius is not the entire story. In July 2001, astronomers Guillermo Gonzalez, Donald Brownlee and Peter D. Ward—all from the University of Washington—published a paper in Icarus in which they looked at a much bigger picture.

The Elements of the Galaxy

The paper presents a study of how the Milky Way's chemical evolution possibly constrains the existence

of earthlike planets in the galaxy. Stellar birth and death ultimately determine when and where chemical elements exist within galaxies. Some astronomers, like Gonzales, contend that earthlike planets can only form if interstellar birth clouds contain the "right stuff." And this notion is crucial to the development of GHZ theory—the chemical compositions of stars, and therefore planets, are intimately linked to galactic location.

The first stars ever consisted of little more than hydrogen, helium, and lithium—the main elements created in the Big Bang. When these seminal stars died, the elements forged within them through stellar nucleosynthesis—the nuclear reactions that keep stars balanced against gravitational collapse—were jettisoned into space. Later stars that formed from these ashes thus incorporated large quantities of heavier elements, or metals. As time goes on more and more stars die and pave the way for new stars, which then contain ever-higher metallicities. As a result of all this plus the gravitational dynamics of the Milky Way, our galaxy is now composed of four distinct components, each of which contain distinct stellar populations. The region where the sun resides is known as the thin disk—a flat pancake about 600 light-years thick—inside of which star formation is still active, and young, metal-rich stars abound. The second component, the thick disk, is about three times thicker and holds older stars containing fewer metals. The bulge that resides at the center of the galaxy is the third component. It contains a mixture of both young and new stars. Lastly, a halo of spherical star clusters surrounds the disk. These globular clusters contain the oldest and most metal-poor stars in the Milky Way, and harbor little, if any, star-producing nebulae.

The fact that stellar metal content, or "metallicity," is correlated with position and time within the galaxy is a key factor in the team's concept of a GHZ. Planets form at the same time as their parent stars, and thus reflect the metallicity of the nebulae that forge them. And, like stars, planets will also have compositions dependent on where and when they form within the galaxy. Old stars—formed from ancient material very poor in metals—ought to breed relatively low-mass terrestrial planets. Conversely, more recent generations of stars—formed from relatively metal-rich nebulae—should harbor comparatively high-mass terrestrial planets. With this in mind, Gonzalez and his team entertained the issue of where among our galaxy's hundreds of billions of stars habitable planets would most likely arise.

Defining the Zone

Astronomers can narrow down the GHZ based on what they know about stars in various parts of the Milky Way. The stars in the halo and the thick disk may simply be too old to hold sufficient quantities of metals for any earthlike planets. With such a low metallicity, any terrestrial worlds that form will be small. These mini-worlds will cool quickly, develop thick crusts, and lack

sufficient gravity to hold substantial atmospheres. A scant atmosphere wouldn't hold enough ozone to protect life from ultraviolet radiation, as is the case on Mars. And with a thicker crust, plate tectonics would not operate and the climate—whose long-term stability depends on the removal of carbon dioxide from the atmosphere by the subduction of surface rocks driven by plate movement—might become too unbalanced. So if the halo and thick disk stars are not made of just the right stuff, this leaves the bulge and the thin disk as the most likely territory for terrestrial worlds.

But according to Gonzalez and his team, they can pin down the GHZ still more precisely. Closer to the galactic core, stellar densities are higher, meaning that any stars there will undergo regular gravitational perturbations. And as we saw earlier, this could mean serious impact hazards for planets orbiting stars that are surrounded by cometary clouds. But perhaps more importantly, being up close and personal to overpopulated star systems also invites danger in the form of radiation from stellar winds, supernovae, or anti-matter and gamma-ray bursts emitted by the supermassive black hole residing in the Milky Way's nucleus. So Gonzalez excludes the bulge from the GHZ.

We are now left with only the thin disk, but not the whole of it. As you move along the disk toward the bulge, star formation rates increase and metals become correspondingly more abundant—because with higher rates of star formation the recycling by nucleosynthesis is much faster. High-metallicity stars, in contrast to low-metal ones, form terrestrial planets that are too massive. Such monstrous planets naturally have more materials to work with—more iron for their cores and more water for their oceans. And due to differentiation, heavier metals like iron would sink to the planetary core while lighter substances like water would remain on the planet's surface or in the atmosphere. Consequently, if Earth, for example, were twice its radius, it would become a water world. Only Kevin Costner would feel at home on such a planet. Gonzalez thinks a world that's too sopping wet inhibits the development of complex life forms because the interaction of land and sea is—like tectonics—a crucial factor in habitable climate control.

So, close to the bulge is not lively real estate. And conversely, as we move toward the edge of the galaxy, far away from the core, stellar densities drop, as does the star formation rate and therefore metallicity. These stars, just like those in the halo and thick disk, will form planets too tiny to host the evolution of complex life.

All this suggests that the stars most likely to support earthlike worlds lie in the thin disk, more specifically in an annulus (the inside of which is roughly 15,000 light-years from the galactic core, and the outside nearly 40,000 light-years) centered on the galactic core and encompassing the sun's orbit (with a mean distance of 28,000 light-years). This, then, is what Gonzalez and his team consider the true Galactic Habitable Zone: The stars here are Goldilocks stars.

They are far from the hustle and bustle of the galactic core, and have metallicities that are just right—not too low and not too high.

The Extent of the Zone

There is not a great deal of evidence for GHZ theory because there are so many variables that come into play. Still, there is one interesting fact that supports the theory: Of all the stars so far found to harbor planets, almost none has less than 40 percent of the sun's metallicity. It was Gonzalez who found this correlation between planetary presence and high stellar metallicity. Some scientists think that these stars have high metallicities because they have swallowed planets that migrated inward, but that would require an unrealistically large number of kamikaze planets. Another thumbs up for Gonzalez and his team concerns a study made using the Hubble Space Telescope to search for planets that might transit across their parent stars, thereby dimming a star's light enough to reveal their presence. The study in question was concerned only with the stars in the globular cluster 47 Tucanae, which thrive in the halo and therefore outside the purported GHZ. The study found that these stars have metallicities lower than 25 percent solar. As old stars, this is expected. But crucially, not one was found to harbor a planet.

Gonzalez and his colleagues feel that in order for a terrestrial world to support life, its mass must lie within a very narrow range—from one-third to three

Earth masses, possibly narrower still. And their best guess for a range in metallicity for an earthlike planet is between 20 and 200 percent solar. Because the metallicity of stars in the thin disk increases steadily toward the disk's center, this suggests that the GHZ, the region of optimal metallicity, extends for 10,000 or so light-years on either side of the sun's orbit. But, notes Gonzales, "the width of both the CHZ and GHZ will depend on the complexity of life one is discussing. Both are wider for simple life." Note also that the GHZ is time-dependent. As time passes, future generations of stars in the neighborhood of the sun will become more and more metal rich because of nucleosynthesis. As a result, the GHZ migrates outward with time.

The SETI Skeptics

GHZ research might impact the search for extraterrestrial intelligence (SETI), currently conducted at the SETI Institute in northern California. If there truly is a region within the galaxy that optimizes the probability of life-bearing planets then, arguably, the SETI Institute should conduct its searches within this zone.

"At the moment, Project Phoenix looks at sunlike stars that are within 150 light-years. In the next 10 to 20 years, we hope to extend this targeted search to perhaps 1,000 light-years. Even with this far greater reconnaissance, involving millions of stars, we are still looking relatively nearby, and therefore well within the

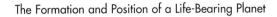

annulus being proposed as most appropriate for ET's abode," explains SETI researcher Seth Shostak. So it seems that at least for right now GHZ research will have little impact on SETI work.

In any case, Frank Drake, the SETI Institute's director, remains unconvinced that the principle of a GHZ has any value whatsoever. "I, and many other people, think the whole thesis of the Galactic Habitable Zone is based on very limited data and much speculation about almost every important issue in the concept," he says. "So little is known about planetary-system evolution and cosmic influences on evolution that it wouldn't be hard to construct an equally appealing scenario almost the reverse of the one being discussed."

Another scientist who prefers a slightly less skeptical approach to the idea of the GHZ is British-born Emma Bakes, an astrophysicist who works for both NASA and the SETI Institute. One of the biggest assumptions that Gonzalez and his team make is that habitable planets will be earthlike, but Bakes feels that it is a mistake to conclude that life requires earthlike conditions. "It is a very shortsighted approach to look for life similar only to terrestrial life," she said. "Even though we use Earth as a paradigm for the blueprints of life, we must not allow it to narrow our vision of what might exist in environments radically different to our own planet. Life could form in giant gaseous planets, which have nowhere near the metal or rock content of the inner terrestrial planets."

Bakes may be correct. Still, we simply don't know if life could exist within the atmosphere of a gas giant. And it's worth noting that even gas giant planets may require high-metal environments in order to form. For example, one theory posits that Jupiter formed when a large planetoid of rock and ice—10 to 20 times the mass of Earth—accreted around the sun and then began to pull in hydrogen and helium by virtue of its enormous gravity. If this is correct, Jupiter too owes its existence to the relatively high metallicity of its birthplace. It is also worth remembering, as already noted above, that virtually all of the gas giant planets found to date orbit stars with substantially high metallicities.

Even if it turns out that planet formation has little to do with metallicity, it remains improbable that life could exist and thrive on a planet, gas giant or not, too close to the galactic core. In short, if there is no outer boundary to the GHZ, there might, at the very least, be an inner one.

Given the number of large planets astronomers have found around other stars, scientists infer that many smaller terrestrial planets also exist. And the ability of microbes to live even in the most extreme environments on Earth leads to the conclusion that simple life may be common in the universe.

But what really captures scientists' imaginations is the possibility of intelligent extraterrestrial life. Are there other civilizations out there? No one knows. Certainly no scientific evidence exists that suggests that such beings have visited Earth, either today or in the past. And searches like the Search for Extraterrestrial Intelligence, or SETI, have so far found no signals emanating from around nearby stars. However, only a tiny fraction of the hundreds of billions of stars in our galaxy have been sampled so far.

The Fermi paradox, attributed to physicist Enrico Fermi in the 1940s, suggests that if advanced life in the galaxy is common, the galaxy is old enough for us to have some evidence of it by now. So where is everybody? Intelligent life may be uncommon in the universe, which would imply that all the factors that influenced life on Earth made it a special place indeed. In this article, Ian Crawford addresses the answers to the paradox and examines the possibility that we are truly alone. —EM

"Where Are They?"
by Ian Crawford
Scientific American, July 2000

How common are other civilizations in the universe? This question has fascinated humanity for centuries, and although we still have no definitive answer, a number of recent developments have brought it once again to the fore. Chief among these is the confirmation, after a long wait and several false starts, that planets exist outside our solar system.

Over the past five years more than three dozen stars like the sun have been found to have Jupiter-mass planets. And even though astronomers have found no Earth-like planets so far, we can now be fairly confident that they also will be plentiful. To the extent that planets are necessary for the origin and evolution of life, these exciting discoveries certainly auger well for the widely held view that life pervades the universe. This view is supported by advances in our understanding of the history of life on Earth, which have highlighted the speed with which life became established on this planet. The oldest direct evidence we have for life on Earth consists of fossilized bacteria in 3.5-billion-year-old rocks from Western Australia, announced in 1993 by J. William Schopf of the University of California at Los Angeles. These organisms were already quite advanced and must themselves have had a long evolutionary history. Thus, the actual origin of life, assuming it to be indigenous to Earth, must have occurred closer to four billion years ago.

Earth itself is only 4.6 billion years old, and the fact that life appeared so quickly in geologic time—probably as soon as conditions had stabilized sufficiently to make it possible—suggests that this step was relatively easy for nature to achieve. Nobel prize–winning biochemist Christian de Duve has gone so far as to conclude, "Life is almost bound to arise . . . wherever physical conditions are similar to those that prevailed on our planet some four billion years ago." So there is every reason to believe that the galaxy is teeming with living things.

Does it follow that technological civilizations are abundant as well? Many people have argued that once primitive life has evolved, natural selection will inevitably cause it to advance toward intelligence and technology. But is this necessarily so? That there might be something wrong with this argument was famously articulated by nuclear physicist Enrico Fermi in 1950. If extraterrestrials are commonplace, he asked, where are they? Should their presence not be obvious? This question has become known as the Fermi Paradox.

This problem really has two aspects: the failure of search for extraterrestrial intelligence (SETI) programs to detect radio transmissions from other civilizations, and the lack of evidence that extraterrestrials have ever visited Earth. The possibility of searching for ETs by radio astronomy was first seriously discussed by physicists Giuseppe Cocconi and Philip Morrison in a famous paper published in the journal *Nature* in 1959. This was followed the next year by the first actual search, Project Ozma, in which Frank D. Drake and his colleagues at the National Radio Astronomy Observatory in Green

Bank, W. Va., listened for signals from two nearby stars. Since then, many other SETI experiments have been performed, and a number of sophisticated searches, both all-sky surveys and targeted searches of hundreds of individual stars, are currently in progress [see "The Search for Extraterrestrial Intelligence," by Carl Sagan and Frank Drake; SCIENTIFIC AMERICAN, May 1975; "Is There Intelligent Life Out There?" by Guillermo A. Lemarchand; SCIENTIFIC AMERICAN PRESENTS: Exploring Intelligence, Winter 1998]. In spite of all this activity, however, researchers have made no positive detections of extraterrestrial signals.

Of course, we are still in the early days of SETI, and the lack of success to date cannot be used to infer that ET civilizations do not exist. The searches have so far covered only a small fraction of the total "parameter space"—that is, the combination of target stars, radio frequencies, power levels and temporal coverage that observers must scan before drawing a definitive conclusion. Nevertheless, initial results are already beginning to place some interesting limits on the prevalence of radio-transmitting civilizations in the galaxy.

The Fermi Paradox becomes evident when one examines some of the assumptions underlying SETI, especially the total number of galactic civilizations, both extant and extinct, that it implicitly assumes. One of the current leaders of the field, Paul Horowitz of Harvard University, has stated that he expects at least one radio-transmitting civilization to reside within 1,000 light-years of the sun, a volume of space that contains roughly a million solar-type stars. If so, something like 1,000 civilizations should inhabit the galaxy as a whole.

This is rather a large number, and unless these civilizations are very long-lived, it implies that a truly enormous number must have risen and fallen over the course of galactic history. (If they are indeed long-lived—if they manage to avoid natural or self-induced catastrophes and to remain detectable with our instruments—that raises other problems, as discussed below.) Statistically, the number of civilizations present at any one time is equal to their rate of formation multiplied by their mean lifetime. One can approximate the formation rate as the total number that have ever appeared divided by the age of the galaxy, roughly 12 billion years. If civilizations form at a constant rate and live an average of 1,000 years each, a total of 12 billion or so technological civilizations must have existed over the history of the galaxy for 1,000 to be extant today. Different assumptions for the formation rate and average lifetime yield different estimates of the number of civilizations, but all are very large numbers. This is what makes the Fermi Paradox so poignant. Would none of these billions of civilizations, not even a single one, have left any evidence of their existence?

Extraterrestrial Migration

This problem was first discussed in detail by astronomer Michael H. Hart and engineer David

Viewing in independent papers, both published in 1975. It was later extended by various researchers, most notably physicist Frank J. Tipler and radio astronomer Ronald N. Bracewell. All have taken as their starting point the lack of clear evidence for extra-terrestrial visits to Earth. Whatever one thinks about UFOs, we can be sure that Earth has not been taken over by an extraterrestrial civilization, as this would have put an end to our own evolution and we would not be here today.

There are only four conceivable ways of recon-ciling the absence of ETs with the widely held view that advanced civilizations are common. Perhaps interstellar spaceflight is infeasible, in which case ETs could never have come here even if they had wanted to. Perhaps ET civilizations are indeed actively explor-ing the galaxy but have not reached us yet. Perhaps interstellar travel is feasible, but ETs choose not to undertake it. Or perhaps ETs have been, or still are, active in Earth's vicinity but have decided not to inter-fere with us. If we can eliminate each of these explanations of the Fermi Paradox, we will have to face the possibility that we are the most advanced life-forms in the galaxy.

The first explanation clearly fails. No known prin-ciple of physics or engineering rules out interstellar spaceflight. Even in these early days of the space age, engineers have envisaged propulsion strategies that might reach 10 to 20 percent of the speed of light, thereby permitting travel to nearby stars in a matter of decades [see "Reaching for the Stars," by Stephanie D. Leifer; SCIENTIFIC AMERICAN, February 1999].

For the same reason, the second explanation is problematic as well. Any civilization with advanced rocket technology would be able to colonize the entire galaxy on a cosmically short timescale. For example, consider a civilization that sends colonists to a few of the planetary systems closest to it. After those colonies have established themselves, they send out secondary colonies of their own, and so on. The number of colonies grows exponentially. A colonization wave front will move outward with a speed determined by the speed of the starships and by the time required by each colony to establish itself. New settlements will quickly fill in the volume of space behind this wave front.

Assuming a typical colony spacing of 10 light-years, a ship speed of 10 percent that of light, and a period of 400 years between the foundation of a colony and its sending out colonies of its own, the colonization wave front will expand at an average speed of 0.02 light-year a year. As the galaxy is 100,000 light-years across, it takes no more than about five million years to colonize it completely. Though a long time in human terms, this is only 0.05 percent of the age of the galaxy. Compared with the other relevant astronomical and biological timescales, it is essentially instantaneous. The greatest uncertainty is the time required for a colony to establish itself and spawn new settlements. A reasonable upper limit might be 5,000 years, the time it has taken human civilization to develop from the earliest cities to spaceflight. In that case, full galactic colonization would take about 50 million years.

The implication is clear: the first technological civilization with the ability and the inclination to colonize the galaxy could have done so before any competitors even had a chance to evolve. In principle, this could have happened billions of years ago, when Earth was inhabited solely by microorganisms and was wide open to interference from outside. Yet no physical artifact, no chemical traces, no obvious biological influence indicates that it has ever been intruded upon. Even if Earth was deliberately seeded with life, as some scientists have speculated, it has been left alone since then.

It follows that any attempt to resolve the Fermi Paradox must rely on assumptions about the behavior of other civilizations. For example, they might destroy themselves first, they might have no interest in colonizing the galaxy, or they might have strong ethical codes against interfering with primitive life-forms. Many SETI researchers, as well as others who are convinced that ET civilizations must be common, tend to dismiss the implications of the Fermi Paradox by an uncritical appeal to one or more of these sociological considerations.

But they face a fundamental problem. These attempted explanations are plausible only if the number of extraterrestrial civilizations is small. If the galaxy has contained millions or billions of technological civilizations, it seems very unlikely that they would all destroy themselves, be content with a sedentary existence, or agree on the same set of ethical rules for the treatment of less developed forms of life. It would take only one technological civilization to embark, for whatever reason, on a program of galactic colonization. Indeed, the only technological civilization we actually know anything about—namely, our own—has yet to self-destruct, shows every sign of being expansionist, and is not especially reticent about interfering with other living things.

Despite the vastness of the endeavor, I think we can identify a number of reasons why a program of interstellar colonization is actually quite likely. For one, a species with a propensity to colonize would enjoy evolutionary advantages on its home planet, and it is not difficult to imagine this biological inheritance being carried over into a space-age culture. Moreover, colonization might be undertaken for political, religious or scientific reasons. The last seems especially probable if we consider that the first civilization to evolve would, by definition, be alone in the galaxy. All its SETI searches would prove negative, and it might initiate a program of systematic interstellar exploration to find out why.

Resolving the Paradox?

Furthermore, no matter how peaceable, sedentary or uninquisitive most ET civilizations may be, ultimately they will all have a motive for interstellar migration, because no star lasts forever. Over the history of the galaxy, hundreds of millions of solar-type stars have run out of hydrogen fuel and ended their days as red giants and white dwarfs. If civilizations were common around such stars, where have they gone? Did they all just allow themselves to become extinct?

The apparent rarity of technological civilizations begs for an explanation. One possibility arises from considering the chemical enrichment of the galaxy. All life on Earth, and indeed any conceivable extraterrestrial biochemistry, depends on elements heavier than hydrogen and helium—principally, carbon, nitrogen and oxygen. These elements, produced by nuclear reactions in stars, have gradually accumulated in the interstellar medium from which new stars and planets form. In the past the concentrations of these elements were lower—possibly too low to permit life to arise. Among stars in our part of the galaxy, the sun has a relatively high abundance of these elements for its age. Perhaps our solar system had a fortuitous head start in the origins and evolution of life.

But this argument is not as compelling as it may at first appear. For one, researchers do not know the critical threshold of heavy-element abundances that life requires. If abundances as low as a tenth of the solar value suffice, as seems plausible, then life could have arisen around much older stars. And although the sun does have a relatively high abundance of heavy elements for its age, it is certainly not unique [see "Here Come the Suns," by George Musser; SCIENTIFIC AMERICAN, May 1999]. Consider the nearby sunlike

star 47 Ursae Majoris, one of the stars around which a Jupiter-mass planet has recently been discovered. This star has the same element abundances as the sun, but its estimated age is seven billion years. Any life that may have arisen in its planetary system should have had a 2.5-billion-year head start on us. Many millions of similarly old and chemically rich stars populate the galaxy, especially toward the center. Thus, the chemical evolution of the galaxy is almost certainly not able to fully account for the Fermi Paradox.

To my mind, the history of life on Earth suggests a more convincing explanation. Living things have existed here almost from the beginning, but multicellular animal life did not appear until about 700 million years ago. For more than three billion years, Earth was inhabited solely by single-celled microorganisms. This time lag seems to imply that the evolution of anything more complicated than a single cell is unlikely. Thus, the transition to multicelled animals might occur on only a tiny fraction of the millions of planets that are inhabited by single-celled organisms.

It could be argued that the long solitude of the bacteria was simply a necessary precursor to the eventual appearance of animal life on Earth. Perhaps it took this long—and will take a comparable length of time on other inhabited planets—for bacterial photosynthesis to produce the quantities of atmospheric oxygen required by more complex forms of life. But even if multicelled life-forms do eventually arise on all life-bearing planets, it still does not follow that these will inevitably lead to intelligent creatures, still less to technological civilizations. As pointed out by Stephen Jay Gould in his book *Wonderful Life,* the evolution of intelligent life depends on a host of essentially random environmental influences.

This contingency is illustrated most clearly by the fate of the dinosaurs. They dominated this planet for 140 million years yet never developed a technological civilization. Without their extinction, the result of a chance event, evolutionary history would have been very different. The evolution of intelligent life on Earth has rested on a large number of chance events, at least some of which had a very low probability. In 1983 physicist Brandon Carter concluded that "civilizations comparable with our own are likely to be exceedingly rare, even if locations as favorable as our own are of common occurrence in the galaxy."

Of course, all these arguments, though in my view persuasive, may turn out to be wide of the mark. In 1853 William Whewell, a prominent protagonist in the extraterrestrial-life debate, observed, "The discussions in which we are engaged belong to the very boundary regions of science, to the frontier where knowledge . . . ends and ignorance begins." In spite of all the advances since Whewell's day, we are in basically the same position today. And the only way to lessen our ignorance is to explore our cosmic surroundings in greater detail.

That means we should continue the SETI programs until either we detect signals or, more likely in my view, we can place tight limits on the number of radio-transmitting civilizations that may have escaped our attention. We should pursue a rigorous program of Mars exploration with the aim of determining whether or not life ever evolved on that planet and, if not, why not. We should press ahead with the development of large space-based instruments capable of detecting Earth-size planets around nearby stars and making spectroscopic searches for signs of life in their atmospheres. And eventually we should develop technologies for interstellar space probes to study the planets around nearby stars.

Only by undertaking such an energetic program of exploration will we reach a fuller understanding of our place in the cosmic scheme of things. If we find no evidence for other technological civilizations, it may become our destiny to embark on the exploration and colonization of the galaxy.

3 The Role of the Sun

Astronomers have known for decades that the last stage of the Sun's life will spell trouble for any life still remaining on Earth. About 5 billion years or so from now, astronomers predict that the Sun will finish burning hydrogen in its core and will swell many, many times its current size into a star called a red giant, possibly engulfing Earth. The details of the next few billion years, however, have become a new focus of research, advanced by powerful computers and robust theories of stellar evolution.

The exact scenario holds a morbid fascination for anyone studying the future of life on Earth, from the exact moment the planet becomes uninhabitable for us to the final question: will Earth be engulfed by the Sun?

Astronomer Mark Garlick explores the future evolution of the Sun and how it will affect life on Earth in this article from Sky & Telescope. —EM

"The Fate of the Earth"
by Mark A. Garlick
Sky & Telescope, October 2002

We live in fruitful times. Since the first bacterial life emerged some 3½ billion years ago, those first simple seeds have evolved into all the incredibly diverse life forms that dwell on and under Earth's surface, swim its seas, and take to its skies.

But here's the bad news: the living Earth is closer to its end than to its beginning. The biosphere is already about three-quarters of the way through its lifespan. Blazing 150 million kilometers away, the Sun grows slightly larger and hotter with every million year tick of the geologic clock. This change may be imperceptible throughout the era of any one species (perhaps including humans), but astronomers assure us that the Sun's ultimate fate is sealed—and, with it, that of our planet.

Just over a billion years from now, life on Earth will begin to perish forever—if it has not already disappeared by then. This might seem like a surprise, because astronomers proclaim that the Sun, at age 4.6 billion years, will not expand to become a red giant for about another 7 billion years. But the Sun's evolution will cause it to bake and sterilize Earth long before then.

In this article, we will see how. We'll look to the deep future and examine the fates of first our planet, and then our star, to the best of our current knowledge. And last, we will look at a surprisingly plausible way to literally move the Earth and keep it comfortably habitable for billions of years beyond its appointed date of demise.

Inside the Sun

The Sun is gradually growing brighter as the result of slow, one-way changes in its core. Like most other stars, the Sun rests in a stable balance between the inward pull of its gravity and the outward pressure of its heat. Gravity tries to collapse the Sun inward, compressing and heating its core to the point that nuclear reactions convert hydrogen into helium. These reactions release heat, which creates enough pressure to hold up the interior against further collapse. Stars in this long, stable phase of their lives lie on what's called the "main sequence" in the Hertzsprung-Russell diagram of stellar brightness versus temperature.

However, the Sun is gradually using up its hydrogen fuel and leaving helium "ash" behind in the core. Four hydrogen nuclei go into the manufacture of one helium nucleus, so the average mass of a particle inside the Sun is growing with time. Yet a helium nucleus exerts no more gas pressure than a hydrogen nucleus does. As a result, the slow conversion of hydrogen to helium alters the balance between pressure and gravity. As time passes, the core shrinks ever so slightly. In this denser, hotter core the nuclear reactions go faster. The increased energy flowing out from the core expands the rest of the star slightly and increases its luminosity.

This slow change has been going on since our star first began to shine. Already the Sun is some 30 percent more luminous than it was 4.6 billion years ago. The trend will continue at an ever increasing pace until the Sun mushrooms enormously to become a red giant. But the brightening will start to wreak serious havoc on our biosphere long before then.

Depletion of Carbon Dioxide

The first scientists to comment on the most immediate effects of the Sun's gradual brightening were James Lovelock (famous for his "Gaia hypothesis," the idea that Earth self-regulates its climate) and Michael Whitfield. Writing in *Nature* in 1982, they showed that as Earth warms up, its surface rocks will weather faster and react more readily with the carbon dioxide in our atmosphere. CO_2 gets removed from the atmosphere and chemically bonded in sediments. Lovelock and Whitfield calculated that, within the alarmingly short span of just 100 million years, atmospheric CO_2 would diminish to levels too low to support photosynthesis. Plants would vanish— spelling disaster for the animals that eat them and breathe their oxygen. And all this, claimed Lovelock and Whitfield, happens in a future hardly farther removed from us than the age of the dinosaurs.

This may seem grim, but current thinking is that Lovelock and Whitfield, though on the right track, were a little pessimistic. Ten years after their work, in 1992, two more scientists published another *Nature* paper in which they performed similar calculations but much more rigorously and realistically. The new model, by Ken Caldeira and James F. Kasting of Pennsylvania State University, included a proper treatment of the greenhouse effect, absent from the earlier work.

77

Moreover, Caldeira and Kasting demonstrated that when you take into account highly evolved plants such as corn, certain other grasses, and other species known as C4 plants, the biosphere survives at least 10 times deeper into the future. The reason is that C4 plants require less than a tenth the CO_2 levels that Lovelock and Whitfield had deemed fatal. So we can all breathe a sigh of relief. Little more work has been done in this field since these two papers, but the current consensus is that Caldeira and Kasting are right.

And of course there will be plenty of time, in the coming hundreds of millions of years, for new plants to evolve that require even less carbon dioxide. On such long time scales, life is incredibly plastic and adaptable.

Still, the biosphere is living on borrowed time. Once the geological clock has advanced a billion or so years into the future, our planet faces a different problem: the greenhouse effect from hell.

Runaway Greenhouse Heating

The well-known greenhouse effect happens because certain gases in our atmosphere (notably CO_2) let sunlight shine down to the ground but block the ground from radiating its infrared heat easily back to space. Heat gets trapped, held in by the atmosphere. As a result Earth is warmer than it would otherwise be. In fact, without its cozy atmosphere our planet would be colder by 350°C (630°F). Scientists today fear that the extra CO_2 and other gases we are pumping into our skies have already begun to warm the planet significantly. The general consensus among atmospheric scientists today is that if we don't reduce CO_2 emissions our grandchildren are likely to face catastrophic climate changes—with new patterns of rainfall, floods, and droughts worldwide, massive ecological disruptions, and rising sea levels for which the world has not planned or built. Having the right amount of greenhouse gas is clearly a good thing.

We've just seen that over millions of years, CO_2 should *decrease* as the expanding Sun heats the rocks of Earth so that they weather faster. Shouldn't this diminish the greenhouse effect under a hotter Sun—a fine example of planetary self-regulation?

It's not that simple. The Sun's gradual brightening, while indeed decreasing atmospheric CO_2 (for a while at least), will, in the end, dramatically increase the atmospheric concentration of another greenhouse gas: water vapor.

In a billion years the Sun will be 10 percent more luminous than now. That may not seem like a great deal—but it is. For with that much extra solar heat, the Earth's polar caps will melt completely and the oceans will not only warm up; they'll begin to evaporate on vast scales. The extra water vapor in the atmosphere will trap more heat— which will make the oceans evaporate still faster—and so on. Instead of regulation, we'll ultimately get just the opposite: a runaway. This sorry situation is known as the moist greenhouse effect, and it is far, far more serious than anything we humans could ever inflict ourselves by our CO_2 abuse.

The changes will be slow at first. But researchers expect greenhouse warming triggered by the brightening Sun to raise our planet's *average* surface temperature to around 50°C (120°F) before the Sun reaches its 6 billionth birthday.

Maybe life will adapt to this just fine. After all, as we survey Earth today from the poles to the equator, we see steadily richer ecologies and thicker jungles as temperature rises (wherever there's sufficient water). Clearly, life likes heat. There's no reason to think this trend stops at the temperature that just happens to be Earth's maximum right now. Maybe, given plenty of time to evolve and adjust, the biosphere will become even more energetic and successful nearly up to the boiling point of water. But beyond that, life is certainly doomed.

Besides, the water may run out long before we reach the boiling point. In the uppermost atmosphere, sunlight breaks down water molecules into oxygen and hydrogen. The hydrogen atoms, being lightweight and thus fast-moving at the high temperatures there, escape into space, never to return. This happens faster as more water vapor fills the atmosphere. The planet's precious inventory of water leaks away.

About 3½ billion years into the future the Sun will be 40 percent more luminous than now. Our planet's entire stock of water will have long since vanished, and Earth's surface, bone dry and cracked open, will be about like Venus is today. With no more water, the carbon dioxide that is now dissolved in our oceans (some 25 to 40 percent of the global inventory) will have only one place to go: into the sky. More atmospheric CO_2 means yet more greenhouse heating. Very high temperatures will soften Earth's crust and accelerate volcanic activity, adding yet more CO_2 to the atmosphere. So another runaway situation is set up. The result is an oven planet not only totally devoid of water but enshrouded in a thick envelope of CO_2. There will be no more biosphere.

Dying Sun

For the next several billion years, the lifeless Earth will see no more major change aside from a steady increase in temperature. But about 7 billion years from now the Sun's output will begin to rise more dramatically, setting the stage for the next phase of solar evolution. By the time our star reaches an age of 12 billion years the hydrogen supply in its core will run out.

At this point the core will begin to collapse, no longer able to hold itself up against gravity. The collapse will boost energy production as it drags fresh hydrogen down to the new, hotter environment. The increased energy output puffs the Sun's outer layers to twice, then three times or more their present diameter. Our star's main-sequence life has ended. The Sun becomes, for about 700 million years, a subgiant.

When all of the hydrogen in the core becomes exhausted, hydrogen burning shifts to an ever-growing shell on the core's outside. This change sets in motion events that greatly speed up hydrogen consumption and energy production, making the Sun's surface layers puff up to truly staggering dimensions. The star grows into a bloated caricature of its former self more than 160 times its current diameter. It has become a red giant.

Vanishing Earth?

At this point the inner solar system is in for a truly bad time. As the red-giant Sun enlarges, it will engulf and vaporize Mercury, then Venus. The solar system's planet count will reduce by two. But what of Earth? The answer here is not clear-cut.

The reason is that the red-giant phase of a star's life involves dramatic mass loss, courtesy of a powerful stellar wind. The Sun is losing material even today, via the solar wind that streams from the outer corona. Currently the Sun is shedding hardly more than a thousandth of a percent of its mass per billion years. But red-giant winds, such as those observed from Mira variables late in the red-giant stages, are much more fearsome. The wind from a red giant ultimately hurls a fair fraction of the star's material into space—indeed, this is how planetary nebulae form. Stellar-evolution models show that the Sun will lose nearly half its mass before it ends up as a white dwarf.

As the Sun sheds mass, the planets will move into larger, wider orbits due to the weakening of the Sun's gravity. This renders Earth's ultimate fate uncertain. Perhaps our planet will barely escape the Sun's expansion by moving out to an orbit somewhere near where Mars is now.

Whether this happens depends on whether the Sun loses enough matter before it gets too big. Some models based on observed stellar mass loss indicate that Earth will indeed have time to escape. But other models predict quite a different result. According to calculations by George Bowen and Lee Anne Wilson at Iowa State University, the final mass-loss episode probably occurs only after the Sun has already swallowed Earth.

Astronomers aren't sure exactly what happens near the end of the red-giant era because no one yet has a convincing model for the events associated with the "helium flash" the first ignition of the helium in the core that's left over from hydrogen burning. When the core becomes hot and dense enough, helium nuclei suddenly fuse to form carbon. Wilson's research leads her to believe that the Sun will probably survive the helium flash with most of its mass intact. Says Wilson, "Earth is incinerated and its ashes are scattered in the final wind of the Sun."

Kacper Rybicki of the Polish Academy of Sciences and Carlo Dens of the University of Liege, Belgium, recently performed a more sophisticated analysis that included tidal effects between our planet and the bloated Sun. Tidal interactions will tend to shrink Earth's orbit. Rybicki and Denis didn't settle the question for sure, but they too believe the giant Sun's outer fringes will most likely snare Earth and drag it in— especially during the last stages of red gianthood, when repeated helium-flash pulses briefly expand our star to its utmost.

Even if Earth does manage to edge out of danger, it is in for a broiling. Its surface temperature is expected to exceed 1,500°C (bright red hot) when the Sun's luminosity peaks at 2,000 to 3,000 times its present value. Earth will be a molten lava ball, with its entire atmosphere—and quite possibly its former crust—boiled away into space.

Save the Earth!

If this all sounds too depressing, good news is at hand in the form of a possible happier ending. According to a team of scientists led by Donald G. Korycansky of the University of California, Santa Cruz, our descendants could preserve Earth's pleasant climate for billions of years beyond the anticipated runaway greenhouse, right up until the Sun becomes a red giant. How? By dragging the entire planet away from the enlarging Sun.

Their proposed method requires remarkably little energy expenditure on our part, considering the size of the job. The method works just like the well-known gravitational slingshot effect, which NASA uses to accelerate spacecraft by means of planetary flybys. As a probe flies through a moving planet's gravitational field, the planet's motion can speed up the probe, slow it down, or redirect it depending on how the encounter is arranged.

Korycansky says the same process could be used to boost Earth to a larger orbit by directing an asteroid or Kuiper Belt object to make repeated close flybys of Earth and Jupiter, arranged just right. In this way the asteroid could transfer orbital energy from Jupiter (which has plenty to spare) to the much lighter Earth, enlarging our orbit slightly with each flyby and tugging us away from the brightening Sun. To direct the asteroid, fuel could be mined on its surface to power some sort of driving mechanism, such as giant rocket engines. Careful use of gravitational perturbations by other planets could do almost all the actual work of positioning the asteroid.

This scheme becomes feasible because of the vast amount of time that's available. According to Korycansky, if a 150-km asteroid were used, just one encounter every 6,000 years could keep Earth edging away from the Sun at the right pace to counteract the Sun's growing luminosity for the rest of its main-sequence lifetime.

Of course there would be dangers. Tweaking a giant asteroid to perform repeated near misses of Earth had better be done exactly right. But if we already have the intelligence to design such an engineering scheme, perhaps putting it into practice will be a walk in the park for our remote descendants. And it certainly beats the alternative—the heat death of Earth in a Venusian greenhouse.

Life owes its very existence to the Sun, from the first microorganisms incubated in Earth's oceans to the plants at the base of the animal food chain. The only life we know of in the

universe is on Earth, where it started and thrives because of the Sun.

The Sun continues to influence daily life on Earth in many ways. Weather systems, including hurricanes and other violent storms, are powered by the radiation from the Sun. Evidence suggests Earth's climate may depend on sunspot cycles, though scientists don't yet know how. Magnetic storms on the Sun release streams of charged particles that can damage satellites and disrupt power grids. These particles also provide the ethereal glow of auroras as they stream onto Earth's poles.

Scientists are starting to understand some of these processes, as this article from National Geographic explains. With a wealth of new data from telescopes and satellites, and the help of powerful computers to model solar physics, scientists are taking their first steps toward understanding the Sun. —EM

From "The Sun: Living with a Stormy Star"
by Curt Suplee
National Geographic, July 2004

Although nearly everything that happens in and on the sun affects our planet, two kinds of explosive solar events impact Earthlings most severely. One is a solar flare, in which a small area above the solar surface suddenly roars to tens of millions of degrees, throwing off a surge of radiation that can cause communications blackouts, disable satellites, or, theoretically, kill a spacewalking astronaut.

The other event is a coronal mass ejection (CME), in which billions of tons of charged particles escape from the sun's halo, the corona, at millions of miles an hour. When these behemoth clouds slam into Earth's protective magnetosphere, they squash the magnetic field lines and dump trillions of watts of power into Earth's upper atmosphere. This can overload power lines, causing massive blackouts, and destroy delicate instruments on anything in Earth's orbit.

Often flares and CMEs occur together; as was the case last October when the fourth most powerful flare ever observed exploded. Back-to-back CMEs then smacked the planet. Thanks to modern detection equipment, we had enough warning to take preventive action. The atmosphere was so electrically charged that the northern lights were seen as far south as the Mediterranean, but little damage was done. By contrast, in 1989, when a fierce CME struck the Earth, it blew out HydroQuebec's power grid, leaving almost seven million people without electricity, and a multimillion-dollar damage bill.

Not surprisingly, locating the causes of such events is a top priority among researchers. But our star has been slow to give up its secrets, and no wonder: To study the sun is to enter a realm that is surpassingly weird.

Most of the Earth is solid. By contrast, all of the sun is gas: about 70 percent hydrogen, 28 percent helium, and 2 percent heavier elements. The outer visible layer is called the photosphere. But in fact, the sun has no "surface," and its atmosphere extends all the way to Earth and beyond, thinning out as it goes.

Moreover, the sun is a madhouse of electromagnetic activity. On Earth very few materials are good conductors of electricity. But in the sun almost everything is electrically conductive because there aren't many intact neutral atoms. The overwhelming thermal and radiation energies excite electrons to the point at which they pop off their atoms, creating a seething stew of positively charged nuclei and free negative electrons—a gaseous mix called plasma that can carry current as easily as copper wire.

Like any electrically charged object, plasma produces magnetic fields when it moves. As those fields shift, they induce more currents to flow, which in turn produce more fields. This tangle of plasma and magnetic and electrical effects determines the forms of nearly everything in or above the sun, such as the bright coronal loops and the dark areas we call sunspots.

"Everything we see as solar activity," says Stephen Keil, director of the National Science Foundation's National Solar Observatory, a consortium of facilities in New Mexico and Arizona, with telescopes around the world, "is a magnetic field being acted on by plasma and vice versa." Both are forever in motion.

The source of this energy is nuclear fusion. Like all stars, the sun formed when local gas and dust drifted together, drawn by gravity, swirling into a sphere. As the mass became larger and larger, hydrogen at the center was crushed by the gigantic pressure, finally sparking a fusion reaction in which hydrogen nuclei come together in a multistep reaction to create helium. The resulting nuclei are just slightly less massive than the component hydrogen nuclei that formed them. The difference is converted to energy according to Einstein's famous $E = mc^2$.

Much of that energy is carried away as light in the form of gamma rays—the most energetic wavelength of electromagnetic radiation. But the solar core is so dense that a single photon, the fundamental unit of light, can't go even a fraction of a millimeter before banging into some subatomic particle, where it is scattered or absorbed and re-emitted. As a result, it can take hundreds of thousands of years for a photon to ricochet its way nearly half a million miles to the sun's surface. By that time, it has shed so much energy that most of it emerges as the fairly puny radiation we call visible light.

It took decades to comprehend the physics of this process, which was ridiculed as outlandish in the 1920s when it was first suggested by the great British astronomer Sir Arthur Eddington and others, who were convinced that the source of the sun's power was some subatomic phenomenon requiring enormous heat. "We do not argue with the critic who urges that the stars are not hot enough for this process," Eddington wrote in 1926. "We tell him to go and find a hotter place."

By the 1950s, however, the fusion model had been convincingly verified, except for one infuriating mystery: the output of wraithlike subatomic particles called neutrinos that are produced in the fusion process. Despite decades of painstaking searches, researchers were able to detect only a third of the neutrinos that theory predicts should strike the Earth every day. Finally, three years ago, a remarkable international effort involving facilities in Japan and Canada solved the problem by demonstrating that the "missing" neutrinos had mutated into different types that had not been detectable until the latest instruments became available. Solar physicists are still rejoicing.

Elation indeed is the feeling in the science community for what today's explorations are adding to our knowledge of the sun. Peter Gilman, a veteran sun researcher with NCAR's High Altitude Observatory, sums it up: "This is the golden age of solar science."

As the neutrino resolution illustrates, it's an international affair. The workhorse of the solar space fleet, for instance, is the Solar and Heliospheric Observatory (SOHO), a satellite ruts jointly by the European Space Agency and NASA. Launched in 1995, its arsenal of instruments has contributed to the research of scientists around the world.

Breakthroughs have been made on all solar fronts. But nearly every hard-won answer has revealed new puzzles: The ceaseless dance between plasma and magnetic fields makes it maddeningly difficult to tease apart cause and effect. Each major level of solar phenomena is influenced by the others, each has a direct effect on Earth, and each is still not completely understood. The momentum toward solving what solar physicists think of as the "big questions" isn't likely to slow, given our ever greater need to predict space weather. And because, as astronomer John Harvey of the National Solar Observatory puts it: "The sun is the only astronomical object that critically matters to humankind." Among the big questions (in no particular order) are:

What interior mechanisms produce the sun's mighty magnetic dynamo?

The magnetic field drives virtually everything on the sun. Our star has an overall main magnetic field, with opposite north and south magnetic poles like the Earth's. Geophysicists believe that the Earth's field is formed by the dynamo-like motion of molten iron in the outer part of our planet's ultrahot core. Similarly, the sun's overarching field seems to be produced by internal motion of plasma.

Until recently, however, it was impossible to see anything beneath the blazing photosphere. Then in the early 1980s scientists developed a technique called helioseismology—a sort of ultrasound scan of the solar innards that allows researchers to analyze the propagation of sound waves through the sun using the techniques geologists use to understand the interior structure of the Earth.

"Nobody dreamed 30 years ago that there would be the possibility of looking beneath the surface of a star" says John Leibacher, program director for the Global Oscillation Network Group (GONG), a worldwide array of automated observation stations funded by the National Science Foundation and positioned about 60 degrees apart around the Earth to view the sun 24 hours a day.

The idea of analyzing sound waves originated in the 1960s, when a Caltech physicist named Robert Leighton used Doppler imaging techniques to show that the solar surface throbbed with rhythmic oscillations like the skin of a drum, with a frequency of about one beat every five minutes. Solar astronomers later found more and different waves that resonate throughout the sun, and in the 1990s began to apply the science of acoustics to data from GONG and from space-based instruments like SOHO. "As a result, we're seeing structures inside the sun that nobody expected," says solar physicist Craig DeForest of Boulder's Southwest Research Institute (SwRI).

Perhaps the biggest surprise is how the innermost layers revolve—especially when compared with the sun's peculiar outer rotation. It takes roughly 26 days from the visible photosphere and the convection zone just below it to make a complete revolution at the equator at about 4,400 mph, but about 36 days near the poles at a sluggish 545 mph.

Many scientists had long suspected that the inner layers of the sun—the core and the vast radiation zone—were spinning faster than the upper layers. That turned out to he partly right. The inner layers are rotating as if they were a solid body, at one revolution per 27 days—slower than the upper layers at the equator butt faster than at the polar regions. That means that the radiation zone and convection zones are spinning at very different rates as they slide past one another. Many experts now think this "shear" area, known as the tachocline, forms the dynamo that generates the sun's main magnetic field.

The internal shearing motion stretches and twists the north-south magnetic field lines, wrapping them around the sun. Doing so adds energy to them, just as stretching a rubber band stores energy in it. Sometimes this action creates powerful ropes of field lines that are buoyant enough to rise. They poke out into the photosphere as loops, prominences, and those enigmatic signposts of solar activity—sunspots.

Why do sunspots fluctuate in 11-year cycles, and what effect does this have on terrestrial climate?

When these titanic bundles of magnetic field lines bulge up and protrude, hernia-like, through the photosphere, they can range in diameter from 1,500 miles to several times the size of the Earth. Sunspots are visible because the bundled field lines impede the flow of convection. The center of the spot, the umbra, appears dark because it's a thousand or more degrees cooler than the surrounding 10,000°F photosphere.

Reliable references to sunspots date from first-century b.c. China, and they were seen by telescope in the early 17th century, but no one made a systematic count until a German astronomer, Samuel Heinrich Schwabe, began a tally in 1826. By 1843 he was confident enough to report that their number goes from minimum to maximum and back to minimum in about a decade's time.

By 1915 American astronomer George Ellery Hale and colleagues at California's Mount Wilson Observatory had shown that the spots usually appear in pairs, aligned roughly parallel to the sun's equator, and that each half of a pair has the opposite magnetic polarity. Further, they determined that all spot pairs in the sun's northern hemisphere have the same orientation and that all the spot pairs in the southern hemisphere have the opposite orientation. Clearly, the arrangement of sunspots is directly influenced by the internal wrapping of the sun's main north-south magnetic field.

Every 11 years, on average, the sun reverses its overall magnetic polarity: Its north magnetic pole becomes a south pole, and vice versa. So a complete magnetic solar cycle—returning the sun to its initial orientation—actually lasts an average of 22 years. No one completely understands the entire process, just as no one understands why the Earth's field also reverses itself at seemingly random intervals, most recently about 780,000 years ago.

That's unfortunate, because there's evidence that sunspot cycles have direct consequences for human life. Witness the sobering case of the Maunder Minimum, the eerie stretch from 1645 to 1715 in which records show that practically no sunspots appeared on the solar face.

It was named after British astronomer E. Walter Maunder, who in the 1890s tried in vain to stir up interest in this aberration. In the 1970s American solar physicist Jack Eddy revisited Maunder's work, noting that the Minimum offered "a good test case for solar influence on climate." Eddy, like most solar scientists at the time, wasn't convinced that variations in sunspot numbers—the most visible indicator of solar activity—had any link to terrestrial climate. He examined data on the growth rings of trees from the 70-year-long minimum. They contained significantly more carbon 14 than trees before and after the period. That meant that higher amounts of cosmic radiation had been reaching Earth during that time. (A magnetically active sun reduces the cosmic radiation we receive.) So, Eddy concluded, there might be a connection after all.

Eddy's investigation also drew attention to another sunspot dearth from 1460 to 1550. Putting that episode next to the Maunder dates, scientists realized that these extended minimums coincided with the core of a famously frigid period in Europe and elsewhere known as the Little Ice Age (1400–1850), during which the Thames River in London and the Lagoon of Venice regularly froze.

It might seem as if fewer sunspots should mean a brighter sun. But the sun's luminosity is actually greater when there are more sunspots, because their magnetism creates extra-bright areas called faculac.

Sunspot activity has indeed been high over the past century as Earth's temperatures have climbed. But according to a recent NASA report, greater luminosity seems to account for only half of the global temperature increase before 1940, and less than that in later years as greenhouse gases have continued to rise. Swings in solar activity are only part of the puzzle.

Moreover, our knowledge of those swings is limited. Our best helioseismological studies and high-tech spacecraft observations only cover about 15 years. And as Joel B. Mozer, senior physicist at the Air Force Research Laboratory at Sacramento Peak, New Mexico, points out, "Since the beginning of the space age in the 1950s, we've had only four solar cycles. All our understanding is based on that. But there's plenty of evidence that these don't represent the extremes."

From computer simulations, scientists have a fair idea of how sunspots might arise and dissipate. But there are still too few highly detailed observations to compare with theory.

"The hope is that helioseismology will eventually give tins better magnetic field observations at crucial depths says Spiro Antiochos of the Naval Research Laboratory in Washington, D.C., who models the physics of solar outbursts. "Now we have to infer from the surface what's going on below. Even the simple question of the structure of the magnetic field under a sunspot—we just don't know."

How is it possible that the corona—the ultra rarefied halo of ions that extends millions of miles into the chill of space—is typically hundreds of times hotter than the solar surface?

For the most awesome extremes of solar output, scientists look to the most inscrutable of the sun's features: the corona. Invisible except during a total eclipse, the corona and its lower altitude neighbor, the chromosphere—a 1,500-mile-thick band of plasma just above the visible photosphere—utterly defy the common-sense assumption that things ought to be cooler if they're farther from the surface of the sun.

The chromosphere is only one-millionth as dense as the photosphere. The corona is one-hundredth as dense as that. And yet, between the photosphere and the corona, "the proportional contrast in temperatures is about the same as if you were standing with your feet in liquid helium and your head encased in a blast furnace," says SwRI physicist Craig DeForest. The photosphere is about 5,700°C, the chromosphere averages 10,000°C, and temperatures in the corona regularly top two million.

Where is that stupendous heat coming from? The leading suspect is a process called magnetic reconnection, a splicing of magnetic field lines that causes energy to be released.

"A key SOHO discovery was that small-scale magnetic fields are constantly generated all over the sun just under the surface," says SOHO's U.S. project scientist Joseph Gurman of NASA's Goddard Space Flight Center. This "magnetic carpet" is made up of small loops arcing up from the photosphere. The bases of the loops are pushed around by plasma. When two lines are shoved together, their stored electrical energy grows to unmaintainable levels. The lines break and reconnect with each other to form a lower energy configuration. The excess energy—sometimes billions of kilowatt-hours—is released in an instant.

"After decades of not being able to come up with enough energy for a coronal-heating model" says Gurman, "we now have a thousand times more energy than needed."

What explains flares and the coronal mass ejections that are responsible for electrical tempests on Earth? How can these storms be predicted?

The corona can produce what Robert Lin, professor of physics at the University of California at Berkeley, calls "the most powerful particle accelerators in the solar system—flares and CMEs. The biggest flares are equivalent to billions of megatons of TNT, all on a timescale of 10 to 1,000 seconds."

Flares expel much of their energy as x-rays and are presumably generated when electrical currents are suddenly released as one or more magnetic field loops in the corona become strained to the breaking point and snap into a new shape. Traveling at the speed of light, the radiation reaches Earth in eight minutes and can disrupt radio communications and navigation systems. A small percentage of flares also hurl fast-moving high-energy protons that can cripple satellites.

But most of the four-alarm worry in the space weather community is devoted to CMEs and their particle barrage. Although CMEs often follow flares, these massive eruptions of plasma also frequently occur on their own. "CMEs fluctuate by many orders of magnitude," says Joel Mozer, the Air Force Research Lab physicist, "and their flavor and character vary."

They ordinarily take one to three days to reach Earth, where they smash into the planet's magnetosphere, deforming it and—if circumstances are right—producing a multimillion-ampere ring current in the belts of charged particles that continually circle the Earth. Even more threatening to communications satellites than flares, CMEs can also take out terrestrial power grids, leaving us in the dark.

It's still not possible to predict when or if CMEs will erupt, because the trigger mechanism isn't known. But with SOHO and other satellites now constantly monitoring solar activity, "we can see these storms leaving the sun in a way we never could before," says Joseph Kunches, chief of space weather operations at the National Oceanic and Atmospheric Administration's Space Environment Center in Bouldler. "We can predict with 80 percent accuracy whether or not they will hit the Earth."

Space meteorologists are also getting at least some warning on the velocity and magnetic orientation of the ejection. The magnetic polarity of a CME can change during its journey. If the polarity is the opposite of Earth's, it does the most damage on impact because the collision of opposite-moving field lines produces enormous charges. Scientists get those readings only an hour or less before a CME strikes, when it passes a satellite called the Advanced Composition Explorer, or ACE. Like SOHO, ACE orbits around a fixed point in space a million miles from Earth, and is built to weather the storm.

The worst storms often come in the waning years after the solar maximum. The most recent solar max ended in 2001; November 2003 marked the strongest x-ray flare ever observed.

Scientists have been measuring flares for only a few decades, and CMEs weren't even identified until the early 1970s. Have we really seen the outermost limits of what the sun can do? We can't be sure. But by the time the next solar max rolls around—seven or so years from now—a new generation of solar observatories will be watching our stormy star, building on an era that for solar physicists has amounted to 20 years of good seeing.

Reprinted with permission from *National Geographic*.

Protected by the Atmosphere

4

Earth's atmosphere is crucial to life on the planet for several reasons. Of course, it provides the air we breathe. It also shields us from dangerous radiation from the Sun and the galaxy. Finally, it causes Earth to maintain a temperature warm enough to sustain life. This last reason is known as the greenhouse effect, and it played a crucial role in life's early history.

As sunlight strikes Earth's surface, light is either reflected or absorbed. Light that is absorbed warms the surface. The surface then cools by emitting heat energy in the form of infrared light.

In a greenhouse, this infrared light is trapped by glass panels, which can be opened to regulate the temperature within. In Earth's atmosphere, the warming process is different. Molecules of naturally occurring "greenhouse gases," such as water vapor, carbon dioxide, and methane, are very sensitive to infrared light. They absorb and then re-release it to be absorbed by another molecule. Eventually, the *heat escapes into space, but the motion of the molecules as they absorb this energy make the air warmer near Earth's surface.*

The following article examines the role of greenhouse gases, particularly methane, in making the young Earth warm enough for water to exist as a liquid, promoting the start of life at a time when the Sun was 30 percent fainter than it is today. —EM

"Goldilocks & The Three Planets"
by Naomi Lubick
Astronomy, July 2003

The idea of greenhouse gases—carbon dioxide, chloro-fluorocarbons, Freon, methane—brings to mind images of carbon based pollutants billowing from industrial, smokestacks, holes in the ozone, snowless winters, and rising ocean levels. While these gases may be negatively impacting life today, historically they may have been responsible for creating an Earth capable of sustaining life.

For the past several decades, carbon dioxide (CO_2) has dominated the atmospheric models for Earth and its nearby rocky neighbors, Mars and Venus. Carbon dioxide has even been used to explain how our Goldilocks Earth became a habitable planet, while too cold Mars and too hot Venus did not. Recently, however, researchers have begun to reassess the prominence of carbon dioxide in the development of the early atmosphere of our planet.

Atmospheric chemists and geophysicists are now turning to an idea that fell out of vogue in the 1970s: the dominance of methane (CH_4) in the early Earth's atmosphere and perhaps in the atmosphere of Mars as well. This smelly gas, more often associated with cows than with evolution, is coming back into style as the molecule of choice for making warm, moist environments suitable for life as we know it.

Methane's stardom in this planetary fairy tale began in the 1950s, in a paper by Carl Sagan and his coworkers, who proposed that the gas could have made the temperature of our planet "just right." Initial models of carbon dioxide-based environments contradicted Sagan's work. But from those models, some of the same researchers are now coming to believe that methane may have dominated in creating Earth's modern atmosphere. Along the way, the same gases that make this planet livable failed to warm Mars and overheated Venus, making Earth the only local world just right for life.

Once Upon a Time

Life on Earth formed from carbon-based organic molecules—the same carbon, hydrogen, and oxygen atoms that make up greenhouse gases also make up our bodies. In the 1950s, University of Chicago graduate student Stanley Miller suggested that the early Earth had an atmosphere of methane and ammonia (NH_3), and that organic molecules formed in this environment could be the precursors of life. Carl Sagan and his coworkers took this one step further and proposed that atmospheric methane could maintain a warm, moist environment conducive to sustaining that life.

In the 1970s, many scientists rejected these ideas; methane's atmospheric life expectancy was considered too short to impact the environment. In sunlight, methane is broken down by hydroxyl radicals. This process, called photolysis, destroys methane in oxygenated environments.

While methane absorbs heat about 30 times more efficiently than carbon dioxide, researchers at the time thought that its transitory nature caused methane to have less of an overall effect than long-lasting, atmospheric carbon dioxide. In today's oxygen-rich atmosphere, methane molecules survive for only about 10 years. In the early Earth's atmosphere, which had less oxygen, methane molecules were estimated to last for about 300 years, but geologically, that's still a short time. Once carbon dioxide is in the atmosphere, it's stable and it's there to stay. Methane naysayers pointed to Venus and Mars, and their modern carbon dioxide atmospheres, and declared carbon dioxide to be the more important molecule.

Where Has All the Carbon Gone?

To prove the dominance of carbon dioxide, atmospheric scientists sought to recreate the atmospheric history of Earth using computer models. In the mid-1980s, James Kasting, a professor at Pennsylvania State University, presented pioneering work on carbon dioxide-based greenhouse atmospheres for Mars and Earth. These models took into account the chemical and temperature evolution of our planet and sought to recreate today's atmosphere via millions of years of evolution.

While Kasting's initial models were promising, problems arose over time that couldn't be ignored. Kasting and other atmospheric modelers were unable to synthesize an atmosphere that maintained temperatures above the freezing point of water without introducing massive amounts of carbon dioxide into their model atmospheres. Pumping the levels of atmospheric carbon dioxide extremely high, however, triggers feedback loops that cause it to condense out of the atmosphere in rain.

While carbon dioxide is chemically stable in the atmosphere, it isn't necessarily permanent. Carbon dioxide can be washed out of the atmosphere in rain, and increasing the atmospheric carbon dioxide level causes it to rain more, which then increases the wash-out rate. Rainwater carries carbon dioxide through the geologic cycle until it gets locked into sedimentary deposits called carbonates. Through erosion and plate tectonics—the motion of Earth's crustal plates—this carbon dioxide returns very slowly to the atmosphere. Since this feedback loop can remove carbon dioxide from the atmosphere faster than the rate Earth can release it, any past peaks in atmospheric carbon dioxide should still be locked away in sedimentary deposits, or at least have left some kind of signal in the geologic record.

Alex Pavlov, a colleague of Kasting, has thought hard about carbon dioxide feedback loops. "Climate models predict 20 percent carbon dioxide in the atmosphere to keep surface temperatures high enough [for liquid water]," says Pavlov, who is now a researcher at the University of Colorado. Today, Earth's atmosphere is 78.1 percent nitrogen, 20.9 percent oxygen, 0.9 percent argon, about 360 parts per million (ppm) carbon dioxide, and slightly less than 2 ppm methane. This implies that if the dominant greenhouse gas in the early atmosphere was carbon dioxide, then our atmosphere dramatically evolved from 20 percent carbon dioxide to essentially no carbon dioxide.

If these models are correct, the currently unobserved carbon dioxide should be trapped in the geologic record in the form of siderite—iron carbonate—deposits. "You would expect a lot of siderite," Pavlov continues. But it hasn't been found in ancient soils, leading researchers to hypothesize that there wasn't enough carbon dioxide. This geologic proof has led researchers to think some other gas might be responsible for warming Earth in its youth.

Pavlov started thinking about methane as the alternative gas while starting his career in Russia at a time when the gas was not in vogue. "When I came here [to work with Kasting at Penn State], Jim was thinking about it—there are problems with carbon dioxide. It was at the limit of its applicability." Together, the two scientists would look for new solutions based on an old idea.

The Too Faint Sun

Just as Sagan was behind the initial idea of methane as a driving atmospheric gas, he may also be behind its return to popularity. According to Kasting, his personal change in perspective was triggered by data published in a 1997 *Science* article by Sagan and colleague Christopher Chyba. This paper was responsible for reviving the debate about how to warm Earth and Mars with a faint, young Sun.

In 1972, Sagan and George Mullen first wrote about the Faint Young Sun problem in another article in *Science*. When the rocky planets in our solar system began forming, they wrote, the Sun's luminosity was about 30 percent weaker than it is now. With such a low level of sunlight, water could not have remained liquid on any of the planets. Nevertheless, there is evidence that zircon crystals formed 4.4 billion years ago in liquid water on what is now Australia. The existence of those crystals mandates an early terrestrial greenhouse atmosphere capable of increasing the temperature enough to keep water liquid. At the same time, the lack of a siderite-rich geologic record indicates that carbon dioxide couldn't have been the primary temperature-raising gas.

In reexamining how to raise the young Earth's temperature with the added problem of a too-faint Sun, atmospheric scientists reevaluated how long methane was able to survive. Models by Pavlov showed that in an early atmosphere without much oxygen, a methane molecule would escape photolysis for 10,000 times longer than in earlier, oxygenated models. Methane may even have persisted on the order of 10,000 years in an ancient oxygenless (anoxic) atmosphere on Earth. Moreover, flesh rock—young solidifying crust—would absorb much of the carbon dioxide present in the atmosphere, leaving methane to take the lead heating our world.

Metabolizing Methane

A warm, wet planet without much oxygen would be very convenient for life if that life were composed mostly of methanogens. These microbes synthesize carbon dioxide and hydrogen to make methane and water—which fits nicely into a methane-dominant scenario.

Kasting says he also likes a methane-dominated atmosphere on Earth because it works for the "Snowball Earth" scenario. Our planet may have been completely glaciated several times in its history, with ice to the equator, causing it to resemble a giant, orbiting snowball. According to Paul Hoffman and Dan Schrag, two very vocal proponents of the snowball theory, a methane greenhouse may have been the key to getting Earth out of that icy state. For Kasting, this may be the final kicker—if life were primarily made of methanogens, then Earth's early life-forms may have maintained a methane-based atmosphere for a long time through their own biological, methane-producing chemistry.

One other factor helps methane avoid destruction: It forms light-blocking haze.

What researchers did not understand when they first rejected methane as a larger component in early atmospheres, says Chris McKay, an astrobiologist at NASA-Ames, "was that methane could form a haze that could protect it [from photolysis]." Recent observations of Titan, Saturn's methane-rich satellite, make it clear that an organic haze created from methane molecules tops its atmosphere. This haze shields methane in the layers below from destructive sunlight.

Hypothetically, Pavlov says, methane molecules at the top of the early Earth's atmosphere could have created long, organic chains that would collide and grow, forming a similar protective haze. These chains could also, Pavlov says, "make it to sediments and be utilized by the biota as a food source." Or perhaps these chains are the origins of life, as Stanley Miller suggested decades ago.

But how did our world evolve from a methane-based ecology to one dominated by oxygen-requiring life-forms? About 2.2 to 2.45 billion years ago, Earth's geologic record shows a sudden jump to an oxygen-rich atmosphere. So-called red beds deposited in that period show that enough oxygen accumulated to oxidize iron. The change to an oxygen-rich environment may have been driven by a variety of different sources. One theory suggests that cyanobacteria—bacteria that give off oxygen—increased in number to the point that they could saturate our atmosphere with oxygen. With the rise of oxygen, no matter the source, methane-producing microbes and atmospheric methane were all but wiped out.

Meanwhile, on Venus and Mars

But what happened on Venus and Mars? Why is one too hot and the other too cold to sustain life? The answer lies in the initial conditions at the birth of each world. Unfortunately, we don't know enough about the geologic record on either of these planets to say for certain what happened in their past.

What we know of their current conditions shows that the picture is simplest for Venus. McKay says Venus never needed methane to get too warm. Venus seems to have suffered a runaway greenhouse effect based on carbon dioxide. Whatever water may have been present on this green planet remained in its atmosphere instead of raining out. Today, greenhouse gases add more than 500°F to Venus's surface temperature over and above what the Sun's heat provides.

Mars is more complicated. It is possible that Mars may once have had a more temperate climate. Many scientists point to dramatic canyons and scarps on the martian surface and say that liquid water must once have flowed freely on the Red Planet. Owen Brian Toon, from the University of Colorado, and his coworkers, however, suggest that Mars's atmosphere was never warm enough to maintain liquid water on its surface and allow for these features to be created via seasonal rainfall. Rather, their work shows that impacts from meteors may have melted martian ice, allowing transitory rainfall to create its apparently water-carved features.

So, perhaps Mars doesn't require rain from a thicker atmosphere. But if it did have an atmosphere with methane (and methanogens), Mars would have been warm enough to retain liquid water.

McKay calls this a "man-bites-dog" story. If the only source of methane is biological, then liquid water on early Mars was due to the presence of life. "Biology allows for liquid water [via methane]," McKay says. "The dog-bites-man is that liquid water allows for life."

These arguments all factor into the discussion of habitable planets. The Goldilocks paradox asks the basic question: Why is Mars too cold, Venus too hot, and Earth just right for water and life? The basic answer is that Earth was in just the right place—not too close and not too far from the Sun. But that is too simplistic. When considering only its distance from the Sun, even Earth would have been at temperatures below the freezing point of water in its early days because of the Young Faint Sun problem.

If distance isn't enough, a second parameter must be responsible. According to Michael Rampino of New York University, a planet's distance from the Sun and its size together determine if it will be habitable. Rampino uses Earth's Moon as his favorite illustration: The Moon, which is the same distance from the Sun as Earth, is not habitable because it is too small to hold an atmosphere.

"As a planet grows, heat is locked inside," says Rampino. Planets start out hot and that heat powers plate tectonics. Plate tectonics renews Earth's crust through cyclical creation and destruction. At spreading ridges between plates (usually mid-ocean), magma wells to the surface and cools into crust. Old crust is destroyed by subduction, which swallows and transforms plates into the molten-rock mantle. During degassing, greenhouse gases (including carbon dioxide) trapped in the crust escape through volcanoes and at tectonic spreading centers. These spreading centers are often teeming with life, even in the otherwise hostile environment of the deep ocean floor.

"If a planet is too small," Rampino says, "the heat builds up and then escapes to space." Without a hot, liquid, planetary interior, plate tectonics ends and so does the carbon cycle. The crust weathers and ages, and the atmosphere condenses as the entire world cools and dies.

On these three rocky planets, the crust's freshness can be translated from the amount of visible cratering. A myriad of Moon pictures, Mars images from *Mariner*, as well as *Venera* images of Venus have allowed Earth-bound geologists and astronomers to assess the ages of these worlds' surfaces, Mars (and the Moon) seemingly had plate tectonics until recently, as is evidenced by fresh crust on its surface and markings of meteorite impacts. Evidence for plate tectonics is unclear on Venus, despite plenty of volcanism. For now, it appears these bodies are tectonically dead.

Happily Ever After?

At their inceptions, Mars, Venus, and Earth were much different from today. Perhaps warmer, they received less sunlight and had unknown continental topographies. Even the amount of cloud formation may have been different. With so many unknowns, scientists must base their atmospheric simulations on best guesses of initial planetary conditions.

Was Mars once warm, or did asteroid impacts cause temporary rainfall to carve its surface? Differing models lead to similar modern-day results. Exploration of the martian geologic record may someday answer that question, but for now, Mars keeps her secrets to herself.

On Earth, we look up to the sky, as well as down through the sedimentary layers, for answers. Pavlov notes that climate models in use today are tuned to the current atmosphere on Earth. "[The] numerous climate feedbacks indeed work at present," Pavlov says, "but we have no idea how they were supposed to work in ancient times."

"Methane is on the rise in terms of explaining a number of things in geology," Rampino says, including climate change on our own planet. "Carbon dioxide was always the favorite. Methane was ignored. If it can be stable, then it provides a very powerful greenhouse gas."

In a past without oxygen, methane may have been stable. Without evidence for past peaks in carbon dioxide levels, methane is becoming the gas of choice for modeling a warm, moist atmosphere for Earth and perhaps for Mars as well.

But models are not truth, says McKay, and have proven challenging even for our own planet, where geologists actually can field-check them. "I've been in this field for 15 years, and I've seen it go back and forth," he says, with regard to methane's role in the evolution of Earth's atmosphere. "The moral of the story is that we don't really know."

And that is what keeps science interesting: the constant struggle to develop, and sometimes redevelop, theories that answer the questions of origins and evolution. Until scientists can field-check the geology on our neighboring planets, models will have to suffice in solving the Goldilocks paradox and the methane versus carbon dioxide debate.

Reprinted with permission. © 2003 *Astronomy* magazine, Kalmbach Publishing Co.

The free oxygen so abundant in Earth's atmosphere is a telltale sign that life exists here. Because oxygen reacts readily with other atoms through oxidation, it would quickly disappear into other compounds—like iron oxide, or rust—if it weren't continually replenished.

Today, green plants achieve this replenishment through photosynthesis, a process that uses sunlight to convert carbon dioxide into the food plants need and releases oxygen as a waste product. In fact, planned searches for terrestrial planets and life will be looking for oxygen in the atmospheres of any Earth-sized planets discovered.

But what was the atmosphere like before life existed, and by what process did it evolve into the air we breathe today? Scientists also wonder why Earth was warm enough for liquid water to exist, providing a medium in which life could start, despite the Sun being 30 percent fainter than it is today. Greenhouse gases, particularly methane, appear to have played a crucial role.

The research in this article paints a portrait of a young Earth in which methanogens—methane-producing microbes—kept the planet warm until oxygen-producing organisms evolved and displaced them. —EM

"When Methane Made Climate"
by James F. Kasting
Scientific American, July 2004

About 2.3 billion years ago unusual microbes breathed new life into young Planet Earth by filling its skies with oxygen. Without those prolific organisms, called cyanobacteria, most of the life that we see around us would never have evolved.

Now many scientists think another group of single-celled microbes were making the planet habitable long before that time. In this view, oxygen-detesting methanogens reigned supreme during the first two billion years of Earth's history, and the greenhouse effect of the methane they produced had profound consequences for climate.

Scientists first began to suspect methane's dramatic role more than 20 years ago, but only during the past four years have the various pieces of the ancient methane story come together. Computer simulations now reveal that the gas—which survives about 10 years in today's atmosphere—could have endured for as long as 10,000 years in an oxygen-free world. No fossil remains exist from that time, but many microbiologists believe that methanogens were some of the first life-forms to evolve.

In their prime, these microbes could have generated methane in quantities large enough to stave off a global deep freeze. The sun was considerably dimmer then, so the added greenhouse influence of methane could have been exactly what the planet needed to keep warm. But the methanogens did not dominate forever. The plummeting temperatures associated with their fading glory could explain Earth's first global ice age and perhaps others as well.

The prevalence of methane also means that a pinkish-orange haze may have shrouded the planet, as it does Saturn's largest moon, Titan. Although Titan's methane almost certainly comes from a nonbiological source, that moon's similarities to the early Earth could help reveal how greenhouse gases regulated climate in our planet's distant past.

Faint Sun Foiled

When Earth formed some 4.6 billion years ago, the sun burned only 70 percent as brightly as it does today [see "How Climate Evolved on the Terrestrial Planets," by James F. Kasting, Owen B. Toon and James B. Pollack; SCIENTIFIC AMERICAN, February 1988]. Yet the geologic record contains no convincing evidence for widespread glaciation until about 2.3 billion years ago, which means that the planet was probably even warmer than during the modern cycle of ice ages of the past 100,000 years. Thus, not only did greenhouse gases have to make up for a fainter sun, they also had to maintain average temperatures considerably higher than today's.

Methane was far from scientists' first choice as an explanation of how the young Earth avoided a deep freeze. Because ammonia is a much stronger greenhouse gas than methane, Carl Sagan and George H. Mullen of Cornell University suggested in the early 1970s that it was the culprit. But later research showed that the sun's ultraviolet rays rapidly destroy ammonia in an oxygen-free atmosphere. So this explanation did not work.

Another obvious candidate was carbon dioxide (CO_2), one of the primary gases spewing from the volcanoes abundant at that time. Although they debated the details, most scientists assumed for more than 20 years that this gas played the dominant role. In 1995, however, Harvard University researchers uncovered evidence that convinced many people that CO_2 levels were too low to have kept the early Earth warm.

The Harvard team, led by Rob Rye, knew from previous studies that if the atmospheric concentrations of CO_2 had exceeded about eight times the present-day value of around 380 parts per million (ppm), the mineral siderite ($FeCO_3$) would have formed in the top layers of the soil as iron reacted with CO_2 in the oxygen-free air. But when the investigators studied samples of ancient soils from between 2.8 billion and 2.2 billion years ago, they found no trace of siderite. Its absence implied that the CO_2 concentration must have been far less than would have been needed to keep the planet's surface from freezing.

Even before CO_2 lost top billing as the key greenhouse gas, researchers had begun to explore an alternative explanation. By the late 1980s, scientists had learned that methane traps more heat than an equivalent concentration of CO_2 because it absorbs a wider range of wavelengths of Earth's outgoing radiation. But those early studies underestimated methane's influence. My group at Pennsylvania State University turned to methane because we knew that it would have had a much longer lifetime in the ancient atmosphere.

Overview/The Microbe That Roared

- Before about 2.3 billion gears ago, Earth's atmosphere and oceans were virtually devoid of oxygen, making the world a nirvana for oxygen-intolerant microbes such as methanogens.

- Scientists now think that methanogens—so named because they give off methane gas as a waste product—could have filled the ancient skies with nearly 600 times as much methane as they do today.

- That extra methane would have produced a greenhouse effect powerful enough to warm the planet even though the sun burned less brightly at that time. Such was the case until the atmosphere filled with oxygen and drove the methanogens into seclusion.

In today's oxygen-rich atmosphere, the carbon in methane is much happier teaming up with the oxygen in hydroxyl radicals to produce CO_2 and carbon monoxide (CO), releasing water vapor in the process. Consequently, methane remains in the atmosphere a mere 10 years and plays just a bit part in warming the planet. Indeed, the gas exists in minuscule concentrations of only about 1.7 ppm; CO_2 is roughly 220 times as concentrated at the planet's surface and water vapor 6,000 times.

To determine how much higher those methane concentrations must have been to warm the early Earth, my students and I collaborated with researchers from the NASA Ames Research Center to simulate the ancient climate. When we assumed that the sun was 80 percent as bright as today, which is the value expected 2.8 billion years ago, an atmosphere with no methane at all would have had to contain a whopping 20,000 ppm of CO_2 to keep the surface temperature above freezing. That concentration is 50 times as high as modern values and seven times as high as the upper limit on CO_2 that the studies of ancient soils revealed. When the simulations calculated CO_2 at its maximum possible value, the atmosphere required the help of 1,000 ppm of methane to keep the mean surface temperature above freezing— in other words, 0.1 percent of the atmosphere needed to be methane.

Up to the Task?

The early atmosphere could have maintained such high concentrations only if methane was being produced at rates comparable to today. Were primordial methanogens up to the task? My colleagues and I teamed up with microbiologist Janet L. Siefert of Rice University to try to find out.

Biologists have several reasons to suspect that such high methane levels could have been maintained. Siefert and others think that methane-producing microbes were some of the first microorganisms to evolve. They also suggest that methanogens would have filled niches that oxygen producers and sulfate reducers now occupy, giving them a much more prominent biological and climatic role than they have in the modern world.

Methanogens would have thrived in an environment fueled by volcanic eruptions. Many methanogens feed directly on hydrogen gas (H_2) and CO_2 and belch methane as a waste product; others consume acetate and other compounds that form as organic matter decays in the absence of oxygen. That is why today's methanogens can live only in oxygen-free environments such as the stomachs of cows and the mud under flooded rice paddies. On the early Earth, however, the entire atmosphere was devoid of oxygen, and volcanoes released significant amounts of H_2. With no oxygen available to form water, H_2 probably accumulated in the atmosphere and oceans in concentrations high enough for methanogens to use.

Based on these and other considerations, some scientists have proposed that methanogens living on geologically derived hydrogen might form the base of underground microbial ecosystems on Mars and on Jupiter's ice-covered moon, Europa. Indeed, a recent report from the European Space Agency's *Mars Express* spacecraft suggests that the present Martian atmosphere may contain approximately 10 parts per billion of methane. If verified, this finding would be consistent with having methanogens living below the surface of Mars.

Geochemists estimate that on the early Earth H_2 reached concentrations of hundreds to thousands of parts per million—that is, until methanogens evolved and converted most of it to methane. Thermodynamic calculations reveal that if other essential nutrients, such as phosphorus and nitrogen, were available, methanogens would have used most of the available H_2 to make methane. (Most scientists agree that sufficient phosphorus would have come from the chemical breakdown of rocks and that various ocean-dwelling microorganisms were producing plenty of nitrogen.) In this scenario, the methanogens would have yielded the roughly 1,000 ppm of methane called for by the computer models to keep the planet warm.

Even more evidence for the primordial dominance of methanogens surfaced when microbiologists considered how today's methanogens would have reacted to a steamy climate. Most methanogens grow best at temperatures above 40 degrees Celsius; some even prefer at least 85 degrees C. Those that thrive at higher temperatures grow faster, so as the intensifying greenhouse effect raised temperatures at the planet's surface, more of these faster-growing, heat-loving specialists would have survived. As they made up a larger proportion of the methanogen population, more methane molecules would have accumulated in the atmosphere, making the surface temperature still warmer—in fact, hotter than today's climate, despite the dimmer sun.

Smog Saves the Day

As a result of that positive feedback loop, the world could have eventually become such a hothouse that life itself would have been difficult for all but the most extreme heat-loving microbes. This upward spiral could not have continued indefinitely, however. Once atmospheric methane becomes more abundant than CO_2, methane's reaction to sunlight changes. Instead of being oxidized to CO or CO_2, it polymerizes, or links together, to form complex hydrocarbons that then condense into particles, forming an organic haze. Planetary scientists observe a similar haze in the atmosphere of Saturn's largest moon: Titan's atmosphere consists primarily of molecular nitrogen, N_2, along with a small percentage of methane. The scientists hope to learn more when NASA's *Cassini* spacecraft arrives at Saturn in July [see "Saturn at Last!" by Jonathan I. Lunine; SCIENTIFIC AMERICAN, June].

The possible formation of organic haze in Earth's young atmosphere adds a new wrinkle to the climate story. Because they form at high altitudes, these particles have the opposite effect on climate that greenhouse gases do. A greenhouse gas allows most visible solar radiation to pass through, but it absorbs and reradiates outgoing infrared radiation, thereby warming the surface. In contrast, high-altitude organic haze absorbs incoming sunlight and reradiates it back into space, thereby reducing the total amount of radiation that reaches the surface. On Titan, this so-called anti-greenhouse effect cools the surface by seven degrees C or so. A similar haze layer on the ancient Earth would have also cooled the climate, thus shifting the methanogen population back toward those slower-growing species that prefer cooler weather and thereby limiting further increases in methane production. This powerful negative feedback loop would have tended to stabilize Earth's temperature and atmospheric composition at exactly the point at which the layer of organic haze began to form.

Nothing Lasts Forever

Methane-induced smog kept the young Earth comfortably warm—but not forever. Global ice ages occurred at least three times in the period known as the Proterozoic eon, first at 2.3 billion years ago and again at 750 million and 600 million years ago. The circumstances surrounding these glaciations were long unexplained, but the methane hypothesis provides compelling answers here as well.

The first of these glacial periods is often called the Huronian glaciation because it is well exposed in rocks just north of Lake Huron in southern Canada. Like the better-studied late Proterozoic glaciations, the Huronian event appears to have been global, based on interpretations that some of the continents were near the equator at the time ice covered them.

This cold snap formed layers of jumbled rocks and other materials that a glacier carried and then dropped to the ground when the ice melted sometime between 2.45 billion and 2.2 billion years ago. In the older rocks below these glacial deposits are detrital uraninite and pyrite, two minerals considered evidence for very low levels of atmospheric oxygen. Above the glacial layers sits a red sandstone containing hematite—a mineral that forms only under oxygen-rich skies. (Hematite has also been found at the landing site of the Mars rover *Opportunity*. This hematite is gray, however, because the grain size is larger.) The layering of these distinct rock types indicates that the Huronian glaciations occurred precisely when atmospheric oxygen levels first rose.

This apparent coincidence remained unexplained until recently: if we hypothesize that methane kept the ancient climate warm, then we can predict a global ice age at 2.3 billion years ago because it would have been a natural consequence of the rise of oxygen. Many of the methanogens and other anaerobic organisms that dominated the planet before the rise of oxygen would have either perished in this revolution or found themselves confined to increasingly restricted habitats.

Although this finale sounds as if it is the end of the methane story, that is not necessarily the case. Methane never again exerted a dominating effect on climate, but it could still have been an important influence at later times—during the late Proterozoic, for example, when some scientists suggest that the oceans froze over entirely during a series of so-called snowball Earth episodes [see "Snowball Earth," by Paul F. Hoffman and Daniel P. Schrag; SCIENTIFIC AMERICAN, January 2000].

Indeed, methane concentrations could have remained significantly higher than today's during much of the Proterozoic eon, which ended about 600 million years ago, if atmospheric oxygen had continued to be somewhat lower and the deep oceans were still anoxic and low in sulfate, a dissolved salt common in modern seawater. The rate at which methane escaped from the seas to the atmosphere could still have been up to 10 times as high as it is now, and the concentration of methane in the atmosphere could have been as high as 100 ppm. This scenario might explain why the Proterozoic remained ice-free for almost a billion and a half years despite the fact that the sun was still relatively dim. My colleagues and I have speculated that a second rise in atmospheric oxygen, or in dissolved sulfate, could conceivably have triggered the snowball Earth episodes as well—once again by decreasing the warming presence of methane.

Extraterrestrial Methane

As compelling as this story of methanogens once ruling the world may sound, scientists are forced to be content with no direct evidence to back it up.

Finding a rock that contains bubbles of ancient atmosphere would provide absolute proof, but such a revelation is unlikely. The best we can say is that the hypothesis is consistent with several indirect pieces of evidence—most notably, the low atmospheric CO_2 levels inferred from ancient soils and the timing of the first planet-encompassing ice age.

Although we may never be able to verify this hypothesis on Earth, we may be able to test it indirectly by observing Earth-like planets orbiting other stars. Both NASA and the European Space Agency are designing large space-based telescopes to search for Earth-size planets orbiting some 120 nearby stars. If such planets exist, these missions—NASA'S Terrestrial Planet Finder and ESA's Darwin—should be able to scan their atmospheres for the presence of gases that would indicate the existence of life.

Oxygen at any appreciable abundance would almost certainly indicate biology comparable to that of modern Earth, provided that the planet was also endowed with the liquid water necessary for life. High levels of methane, too, would suggest some form of life. As far as we know, on planets with Earth-like surface temperatures only living organisms can produce methane at high levels. The latter discovery might be one of the best ways for scientists to gain a better understanding of what our own planet was like during the nascent stages of its history.

Encounters with Asteroids 5

The atoms and molecules that make up our bodies and everything we see around us on Earth came from the universe. All the hydrogen atoms present in water and in countless other molecules have been around since the beginning of time. So have a small fraction of the helium atoms present today and a smaller fraction of the lithium atoms. All the other atoms in existence were manufactured by stars, either in the interiors, where fusion produces elements as heavy as iron, or in supernovas, massive explosions that produce heavier atoms in a process called neutron capture.

Molecules form in cooler environments. Some of the coolest stars form molecules in their atmospheres, but more complex molecules require the cold depths of interstellar space. In molecular clouds, like the Orion Nebula, astronomers are recognizing an increasing variety of complex carbon-containing organic molecules and even more complicated amino acids, the building blocks of proteins. Many such *molecules have also been found in meteorites, raising the possibility that the stuff of life initially came from beyond Earth. —EM*

"It Came from Outer Space"
by Joe Alper
Astronomy, November 2002

If the fossil record is correct, primitive life appeared on Earth no more than 100 million years after the end of the 500 million-year period of sterilizing, cataclysmic bombardments that shaped our newborn planet. A blink of an eye, really—a time frame that makes it almost impossible to imagine earthly life getting its start nearly 4 billion years ago without some outside help.

But probably not the way that likely popped into your mind. Life did not arrive from space. No microbes on meteorites. No panspermia.

But what did likely come from space were the chemical building blocks of primitive life. "One hundred million years just seems a little short to allow for the creation of both the chemicals of life and life itself, but there wasn't a need for those chemicals to be synthesized here on Earth," asserts astrophysicist Scott Sanford, of NASA's Ames Research Center at Moffet Field in northern California. "Instead, those building blocks were probably part of the enormous tonnage of organic chemicals that arrived during the period of heavy bombardment and that continue to arrive from space even to this day."

That's right. The billions of dust grains that speckle our planet every day dump roughly the weight of three school buses (30 tons, or 27.2 metric tons) of organic debris—stuff with carbon atoms bonded to hydrogen, oxygen, and nitrogen atoms—into Earth's upper atmosphere. The universe, it seems, provides a series of chemical refineries from the build-up of ever heavier elements in stellar nuclear furnaces to the molecular molding that occurs in the interstellar medium. In fact, says physicist-turned astrochemist Hugh Hilt of NASA's Goddard Space Flight Center in Greenbelt, Maryland, "the diversity of chemicals made in space arises in most instances from the exact chemistry that we use in petrochemical processes on Earth to make complex organic molecules."

Indeed, evidence collected over the past decade from a wide range of earthly and stellar sources indicates that space is a place that can't help but make organic chemicals. The implications of this are profound, says Jeffrey Bada, a geochemist at the Scripps Institution for Oceanography in La Jolla, California. "Organic chemistry is ubiquitous in the universe, which suggests that if extraterrestrial sources seeded the early Earth with complex organic chemicals, then the same process is likely to be taking place wherever you have planet formation."

In other words, just as organic chemistry appears to be a constant in the universe, so too might the ability for life to arise. "The jump from organic chemicals to life is huge, but if molecules from space had something to do with the development of life here, then that means they're always available to help with the development of life wherever suitable conditions exist in the universe," says Sandford.

Cooking Up a Chemical Stew

In 1953, two University of Chicago chemists came up with a different, potentially universal explanation for how the chemicals of life could arise on a primordial planet such as Earth in its early days. Two years earlier graduate student Stanley Miller heard a lecture by Harold Urey in which the Nobel laureate suggested the chemicals of life could have arisen on Earth through chemical reactions sparked by lightning. Intrigued by the idea, Miller volunteered to run such an experiment with Urey's guidance.

At the time, scientists believed Earth's early atmosphere was "reducing"; that it was composed of hydrogen-rich chemicals such as methane, ammonia, water, and molecular hydrogen, but devoid of molecular oxygen. Using such a mixture as a primordial atmosphere, Miller set up a closed reaction apparatus in which a flask of boiling water stood in for Earth's early ocean, and a pair of electrodes provided the "lightning." After a few days of lightning strikes, Miller's ocean had become a murky brown, so he stopped the experiment and analyzed the water, only to find large amounts of amino acids in the soup. Other experiments by Miller and Urey, as well as by the then-young Carl Sagan, showed ultraviolet light could replace lightning—a handy experimental twist because planetary scientists were beginning to think that lightning wasn't very common in Earth's early days. Further tinkering with experimental conditions yielded a menagerie of biomolecules such as sugars, nucleic acids, and porphyrins—a major component of blood's oxygen-carrying protein hemoglobin.

Most surprising was how easy these results were to obtain, suggesting that Miller-Urey chemistry could jump-start life under a great variety of conditions. But recent evidence suggests that the early atmospheres of our solar system's inner planets, at least, were never reducing. "If Earth's early atmosphere wasn't reducing, and we really don't think it was, then this chemistry could have never occurred," explains Joseph Nuth III, a chemist at Goddard.

That's not to say, though, that the Miller-Urey conditions couldn't occur somewhere in the universe, or even over some parts of early Earth. "I'm not completely convinced that there weren't Miller-Urey conditions here on Earth, particularly in the vicinity of volcanoes, which probably spewed out methane and ammonia," says Bada. "But if you look at the kinds of organic compounds we find in at least some meteorites, then you have to assume that Miller-Urey type chemistry is occurring somewhere in the interstellar medium because the types of compounds—amino acids and the like—and the amounts of those compounds are strikingly similar."

There is, however, a more serious problem with Miller-Urey type experiments, at least as far as the origin of life on Earth is concerned—they generate only what are known as racemic mixtures of the amino acids. Each amino acid, except for glycine, occurs in two versions that mirror each other's shape, in the same way that our hands are identical but mirror images of each other. All living creatures on Earth use left-handed amino acids to make proteins, but the Miller-Urey experiments produce equal amounts of both forms—so-called racemic mixture. And while Miller, now a chemist at the University of California, San Diego, believes early life somehow selected one form over the other at some point during evolution, nobody has yet been able to demonstrate how this might have occurred.

However, amino acids from other sources—space, perhaps—may have already had such bias. If so, the deck might have been stacked in favor of molecular left-handedness.

All the Stuff of Life from Space

From the earliest days of radio astronomy, astronomers have increasingly observed complex chemicals. At first came simple atoms and molecules, such as hydrogen and helium, carbon and iron, aluminum chloride, and magnesium oxide. But as astrochemists looked further, the list took on a decidedly lopsided look, with molecules containing carbon, hydrogen, oxygen, and nitrogen predominating. And by the time researchers started identifying molecules with seven or more atoms, the list became exclusively organic in nature, just as it is for larger molecules here on Earth.

Today, the list of chemicals detected in space ranges from the amino acid glycine up to complex polycyclic aromatic hydrocarbons (PAHs) similar to those found in coal or heavy petroleum. Astronomers identify these molecules based on their ability to absorb infrared radiation at discrete frequencies. The PAHs, for example, account for what was once known as the Unidentified Infrared Bands (UIBs), a collection of spikes in the infrared spectrum first noted in 1973. Lou Allamandola and his colleagues at NASA-Ames have spent nearly 20 years pinning down the true identity of UIBs as, PAHs through a combination of laboratory syntheses, theoretical predictions, and interstellar observations.

In addition, researchers have isolated a wealth of organic compounds from meteorites, particularly the 4.6 billion-year-old Murchison meteorite, which fell in Australia in 1969, and the similarly aged Orgueil meteorite that struck France in 1864. The compounds obtained from meteorites include almost all of the amino acids found in earthly life, as well as many more that aren't found in Earth's biosphere. They also contain nucleic acids (the building blocks of our genes) and a host of other biologically important compounds such as ketones, carboxylic acids, amines, amides, and quinones—a great variety of organics vital to biochemical reactions.

In 2001 researchers fleshed out the list with the discovery of two additional biomolecules—sugars and pyridine dicarboxylic acids, which are also critical biomolecules. To find sugars, geochemist George Cooper and his colleagues at NASA-Ames use a combination of techniques known as gas chromatography and mass spectroscopy to analyze water extracts of pristine samples removed from the interior of the Murchison meteorite. Gas chromatography separates a complex blend of chemicals into its constituents, while mass spectroscopy yields the identity of each component. The results obtained with these tools show clearly that the meteorites contain many different types of sugars and related compounds known as poly-alcohols, or polyols, at about the same concentrations as the amino acids found in these same meteorites. The researchers also found that the relative amounts of heavy to light carbon and hydrogen atoms with the C13/C12 and deuterium/hydrogen ratios—in the sugars revealed that these molecules came to Earth as part of the meteorite and were not contaminants. These ratios are significantly higher in molecules that originated in the interstellar medium compared to those made on Earth.

Cooper was also part of a team led by Sandra Pizzarello, a chemist at Arizona State University, which has examined samples from a more recent arrival on Earth. On January 18, 2000, at about 8:45 A.M. local time, an asteroid or comet broke up in the sky over British Columbia and showered some 500 fragments onto Tagish Lake in the northern reaches of the province. The Tagish Lake meteorite fragments are a treasure to astrochemists because many pieces were frozen solid in the ice sheet above the water and recovered just a week later by amateur geologist Jim Brook. After finding big pieces of ice containing meteorite fragments, Brook was careful not to handle them with his bare hands, and kept them frozen until he could turn them over to the proper authorities. "This was a very significant find, certainly the most pristine, and we were quite anxious to look at the organic materials in the meteorite," says Pizzarello.

The Tagish Lake meteorite—like both Murchison and Orgueil—belongs to an ancient family of meteorites known as carbonaceous chondrites. These primitive meteorites contain significant amounts of carbon and are thought to provide a snapshot of what our little corner of the universe was like at the time the sun and solar system were forming. Pizzarello, known for her analysis of amino acids in meteorites, was able to procure a pristine 4.5-gram fragment. Together with Cooper and colleagues from NASA, Brown University and the University of Rochester, she identified the organic content of the Tagish Lake meteorite, though not, says Pizzarello, "without a great deal more difficulty than we expected. The analysis has been a hellish ride."

She was shocked by the initial data. "We expected the results from Tagish Lake to look like those from Murchison and Orgueil, but when we looked for amino acids we found almost nothing, and when we looked further for amines and carboxylic acids that are quite abundant in Murchison, we found almost nothing again. I thought this was the biggest letdown of my life," she says.

But then pleasant surprises started coming. "First we found dicarboxylic acids at about the same abundance as we see in Murchison, which is odd because we've always thought that the same chemistry that generates the amino acids in Murchison would have made the dicarboxylic acids," explains Pizzarello. "And then we started finding entire new classes of biologically important molecules, such as phenyl dicarboxylic acids and pyridine derivatives such as nicotinic acid." Carbon isotope analysis confirmed that these molecules were indeed created in space, not on Earth.

The Tagish Lake meteorite appears to have preserved organics that accumulated or developed in the early history of the solar system including bubble-like molecules of pure carbon (fullerenes or "buckyballs") containing the noble gases helium and argon, which exist in ratios not found in any terrestrial sources but in relative quantities similar to those found in interstellar gas and dust clouds—and therefore may reflect an early stage of the evolution of complex carbon compounds in space.

"This is really quite important because it's quite clear that the chemistry of the Tagish Lake meteorite is different from that of Murchison or any of the other meteorites we've studied so far, meaning that Tagish

Lake and these other meteorites formed in different interstellar environments," says Pizzarello. "Our theories of how chemistry takes place [in space] are too general. We need to do some more thinking."

Looking for That Spark

In retrospect, admits Pizzarello, perhaps it should not have come as such a surprise that there might be different mixes of organic compounds made in various interstellar environments. After all, in earthly laboratories small changes in conditions can alter the outcome of most chemical reactions, so the same should be true in space, where chemistry could be happening in environments as diverse as within huge dust clouds or in the immediate vicinity of a newly forming star.

The one thing that nearly all environments would require is enough energy to drive chemical reactions. On Earth most chemical reactions are powered by heat, but based on the results of laboratory experiments, ultraviolet radiation serves the same purpose in the cold of space—even better, since it's a higher energy source.

In the astrochemistry lab at NASA-Ames, Jason Dworkin and colleagues have shown that ultraviolet radiation can power a set of chemical reactions with a surprising outcome. Working at temperatures around 15° above absolute zero (-431°F or -257°C), Dworkin created an interstellar ice analog from a mixture of water, methanol, ammonia and carbon monoxide similar to that found in comets. He then irradiated the mixture with ultraviolet light for two days, which left an oily residue on the surface of the reaction vessel. Assuming his organic goop would contain the usual mix of water-soluble organic compounds that other researchers have created in similar experiments, he dissolved the residue in water and found something unusual—droplets formed. Further analysis showed these droplets were actually tiny circles comprising molecules with a water-soluble head and an oily tail, the same kind of molecules that come together to form cell membranes in all creatures on Earth except viruses. In essence, the NASA-Ames team had shown that a fundamental structure of life, a membrane, could form from chemicals made in the cold of interstellar space.

"This was a remarkable result," says Sandford, who worked with Dworkin on this study. "But it's really just an extension of what we've produced in every mixed ice experiment we've run, which clearly shows that mixtures of simple starting materials can react to make hundreds of new chemicals under the conditions seen in interstellar space," says Sandford.

Chemical cookeries might also happen independent of light-driven reactions. At NASA-Goddard, for example, Hugh Hill and Joe Nuth have been doing chemistry on homemade interstellar dust grains designed to resemble the dust that condenses in the cool atmospheres of old stars. The two chemists make the dust by shooting a cocktail of chemicals through a furnace, where a fluffy "astrophysical dust grain analog" rapidly condenses. "Once we had this silicate dust, we wondered if the metal atoms on the surface of these particles could catalyze chemistry, just as metal atoms catalyze chemistry in the lab," explains Hill.

Several experiments later, with a variety of gaseous mixtures as starting materials, the answer was a resounding yes. "We made amazingly complex mixtures of chemicals, including lots of nitrogen-containing compounds, which in overall terms were quite similar to the complex suite of organics you see in meteorites," says Hill, "and since we didn't have an energy source, the metal atoms on the surface of these particles must have been acting as catalysts."

Pick a Hand

There seems to be little doubt that the dust-filled reaches of space can provide an environment ripe for organic chemistry to take place. There is also good evidence, based on work in many laboratories and from telescopic observations, that dust laden with organics can find its way into comets and other large and small interstellar bodies. These objects then act as chemical shuttles that deliver their payloads to developing and established planets. Taken together, these findings provide good reason to think that the chemicals of life could have come from deep space.

But there's still the issue of handedness, of why life on Earth so overwhelmingly chose left-handed over right-handed molecules. Living organisms have evolved so that they use only left-handed amino acids when they make proteins, but that's because nature makes only left-handed amino acids. It's the classic chicken-and-the-egg question: Did life evolve to use only left-handed amino acids, causing the right-handed forms to gradually fade away, or did life evolve to use left-handed amino acids because those were the most prevalent when life got its start?

If Miller and Urey had been correct, nature would have driven this selective pressure on molecular shape. However, the amino acids in meteorites turn out not to be racemic mixtures. Instead, the left-handed forms predominate—what is known as enantiomeric excess—suggesting that the molecules drove nature's evolution. This evidence comes primarily from work done by Pizzarello, who says this is one of the most important issues when it comes to talking about chemical evolution. "Yes, we find enantiomeric excesses in meteorites, but now we have to explain how that might happen out in the conditions of interstellar space."

Indeed, this is one of the great questions before astrochemists these days. For a few years, it appeared that the natural polarization of ultraviolet light in interstellar space could drive chemistry to favor left-handedness over right-handedness, but recently Pizzarello has found enantiomeric excesses much higher than is theoretically possible with polarized light as the leading factor. One new possibility is that asymmetry results from the metal-catalyzed reactions that occur on dust grains, an idea supported by Hill and Nuth's work, as well as by experiments that Pizzarello and her colleagues perform. For now, at least, space-formed molecules may have tilted the balance at life's beginning, but everyone in the field still considers this an open-ended question.

An Earthly Explanation

That's not to say that everyone agrees that all vital organic chemicals came from space, like manna from heaven. Geophysicist Friedemann Freund, a staff scientist at the SETI Institute who spends most of his time at NASA-Ames, is one who thinks he has found a closer source of biological molecules—the magma that flows from volcanoes. Freund has studied the chemistry of microscopic impurities trapped in magma as it crystallizes after a volcanic eruption and detected the characteristic infrared signature of organic compounds. In addition, he has found tiny amounts of water trapped within the magnesium oxide crystals in magma, a somewhat surprising finding but important, he thinks, for the production of organics within cooling magma.

"Within the crystal structure, water can act as a source of peroxide, which can react with trapped carbon dioxide and hydrogen gas to create simple organics," explains Freund, who has done theoretical modeling and laboratory experiments to show this is plausible. He also proposes that as the cooled magma erodes through normal weathering processes, these simple hydrocarbons would react with one another in the presence of the metal-laden crystals acting as catalysts to produce larger, more complex organics. A preference of left-handedness over right-handedness could have resulted, he says, in much the same way that it might arise from metal-catalyzed reactions in space. "And since a significant amount of volcanic rock erodes each year," argues Freund, "magma could have provided just as much organic material to the prebiotic chemical soup as Space-generated organics." In fact, Freund suspects that earthly life got its start thanks to a dual contribution of interstellar and magma-generated organics.

Making the Leap

Did life on Earth get a boost from the stars? While it's impossible to say for certain, researchers do feel confident in drawing one conclusion from these and other studies. "The diversity of organic compounds that we find everywhere we look makes it reasonable to assume that if life has developed elsewhere in the universe, it's likely to be based on pretty much the same biochemistry that has evolved here on Earth," says Sandford. But as Hill cautions, "Creating a prebiotic soup seems fairly easy. But making the leap to life is a huge one."

Scientists know that water was a crucial ingredient in the rise of life on Earth, but where did that water come from? In the solar nebula, as the Sun and planets were forming, scientists believe that

a "frost line" existed beyond the orbit of Mars, inside of which the solar system was too warm for ices to exist. Beyond the frost line, water, methane, ammonia, and other molecules condensed and froze. These ices probably make up a large fraction of the cores of the Jovian planets, Jupiter, Saturn, Uranus, and Neptune. Much of the ice is frozen today in comets, while some of it is locked up in the rocky bodies of the outer asteroid belt.

Scientists suspect that Earth's water was delivered from comets or asteroids during the period of heavy bombardment soon after the planets had formed, when the solar system was being swept free of its larger debris. All the planets were pelted during this period (a few bodies, like the Moon and Mercury, still have the scars to prove it). Some of the incoming chunks would have been water ice that vaporized into the atmosphere on impact, condensing later into droplets and rainfall, as emphasized in this article. —EM

"The Origins of Water on Earth"
by James F. Kasting
Scientific American, September 2003

Of all the planets, why is Earth the only one fit for life? Simple: because Earth has a surface that supports liquid water, the magic elixir required by all living things. Some scientists speculate that forms of life that do not require water might exist elsewhere in the universe. But I would guess not. The long molecular chains and complex branching structures of carbon make this element the ideal chemical backbone for life, and water is the ideal solvent in which carbon-based chemistry can proceed.

Given this special connection between water and life, many investigators have lately focused their attention on one of Jupiter's moons, Europa. Astronomers believe this small world may possess an ocean of liquid water underneath its globe-encircling crust of ice. NASA researchers are making plans to measure the thickness of ice on Europa using radar and, eventually, to drill through that layer should it prove thin enough.

The environment of Europa differs dramatically from conditions on Earth, so there is no reason to suppose that life must have evolved there. But the very existence of water on Europa provides sufficient motivation for sending a spacecraft to search for extra-terrestrial organisms. Even if that probing finds nothing alive, the effort may help answer a question closer to home: Where did water on Earth come from?

Water from Heaven

Creation of the modern oceans required two obvious ingredients: water and a container in which to hold it. The ocean basins owe their origins, as well as their present configuration, to plate tectonics. This heat-driven convection churns the mantle of Earth—the region between the crust and core—and results in the separation of two kinds of material near the surface. Lighter, less dense granitic rock makes up the continents, which float like sponges in the bath over denser, heavier basalt, which forms the ocean basins.

Scientists cannot determine with certainty exactly when these depressions filled or from where the water came, because there is no geologic record of the formative years of Earth. Dating of meteorites shows that the solar system is about 4.6 billion years old, and Earth appears to be approximately the same age. The oldest sedimentary rocks—those that formed by processes requiring liquid water—are only about 3.9 billion years old. But there are crystals of zirconium silicate, called zircons, that formed 4.4 billion years ago and whose oxygen isotopic composition indicates that liquid water was present then. So water has been on Earth's surface throughout most of its history.

Kevin J. Zahnle, an astronomer at the NASA Ames Research Center, suggests that the primordial Earth was like a bucket. In his view, water was added not with a ladle but with a firehose. He proposes that icy clumps of material collided with Earth during the initial formation of the planet, injecting huge quantities of water into the atmosphere in the form of steam.

Much of this water streamed skyward through holes in the atmosphere blasted open by these icy planetesimals themselves. Many of the water molecules (H_2O) were split apart by ultraviolet radiation from the sun. But enough of the initial steam in the atmosphere survived and condensed to form sizable oceans when the planet eventually cooled.

No one knows how much water rained down on the planet at the time. But suppose the bombarding planetesimals resembled the most abundant type of meteorite (called ordinary chondrite), which contains about 0.1 percent water by weight. An Earth composed entirely of this kind of rubble would therefore have started with 0.1 percent water—at least four times the amount now held in the oceans. So three quarters of this water has since disappeared. Perhaps half an ocean of the moisture became trapped within minerals of the mantle. Water may also have taken up residence in Earth's dense iron core, which contains some relatively light elements, including, most probably, hydrogen.

The initial influx of meteoric material probably endowed Earth with more than enough water for the oceans. Indeed, that bombardment lasted a long time: from 4.5 billion to 3.8 billion years ago, a time called, naturally enough, the heavy bombardment period.

Where these hefty bodies came from is still a mystery. They may have originated in the asteroid belt, which is located between the orbits of Mars and Jupiter. The rocky masses in the outer parts of the belt may hold up to 20 percent water. Alternatively, if the late-arriving bodies came from beyond the orbit of Jupiter, they would have resembled another water-bearing candidate—comets.

Comets are often described as dirty cosmic snowballs: half ice, half dust. Christopher F. Chyba, a planetary scientist at the University of Arizona, estimates that if only 25 percent of the bodies that hit Earth during the heavy bombardment period were comets, they could have accounted for all the water in the modern oceans. This theory is attractive because it could explain the extended period of heavy bombardment: bodies originating in the Uranus-Neptune region would have taken longer to be swept up by planets, so the volley of impacts on Earth would have stretched over hundreds of millions of years.

Alternatively, the impactors may have come from the asteroid belt region between 2.0 astronomical units (AU, the mean distance from Earth to the sun) and 3.5 AU. Alessandro Morbidelli of the Observatory of the Côte d'Azur in France and his co-workers have shown that asteroids whose orbits were highly inclined to the plane of the solar system could have continued to pelt Earth for a similar period.

This widely accepted theory of an ancient cometary firehose has recently hit a major snag. Astronomers have found that three comets—Halley, Hyakutake and Hale-Bopp—have a high percentage of deuterium, a form of hydrogen that contains a neutron as well as a proton in its nucleus. Compared with normal hydrogen, deuterium is twice as abundant in these comets as it is in seawater. One can imagine that the oceans might now hold proportionately more deuterium than the cometary ices from which they formed, because normal hydrogen, being lighter, might escape the tug of gravity more easily and be lost to space. But it is difficult to see how the oceans could contain proportionately less deuterium. If these three comets are representative of those that struck here in the past, then most of the water on Earth must have come from elsewhere.

A controversial idea based on observations from satellites suggests that about 20 small (house-size) comets bombard Earth every minute. This rate, which is fast enough to fill the entire ocean over the lifetime of Earth, implies that the ocean is still growing. This much debated theory, championed by Louis A. Frank of the University of Iowa, raises many unanswered questions, among them: Why do the objects not show up on radar? Why do they break up at high altitude? And the deuterium paradox remains, unless these "cometesimals" contain less deuterium than their larger cousins.

More recently, Morbidelli has argued convincingly that most of Earth's water came from the asteroid belt. The ordinary chondrites are thought to come from the inner part of this region (2.0 to 2.5 AU). But outer-belt asteroids (2.5 to 3.5 AU) are thought to be water-rich. According to Morbidelli, as Earth formed it collided with one or more large planetesimals from the outer belt. Gravitational perturbations caused by Jupiter elongated the planetesimal's orbit, allowing it to pass within Earth's orbit. Earth may have picked up additional water from asteroids on highly inclined orbits that arrived during the heavy bombardment period. In this scheme, no more than 10 percent of Earth's water came from comets that originated farther out in the solar system. This theory is consistent with deuterium-hydrogen ratios, which indicate that the comets' watery contributions were small.

The Habitable Zone

Whatever the source, plenty of water fell to Earth early in its life. But simply adding water to an evolving planet does not ensure the development of a persistent ocean. Venus was probably also wet when it formed, but its surface is completely parched today.

How that drying came about is easy to understand: sunshine on Venus must have once been intense enough to create a warm, moist lower atmosphere and to support an appreciable amount of water in the upper atmosphere as well. As a result, water on the surface of Venus evaporated and traveled high into the sky, where ultraviolet light broke the molecules of H_2O apart and allowed hydrogen to escape into space. Thus, this key component of water on Venus took a one-way route: up and out.

This sunshine-induced exodus implies that there is a critical inner boundary to the habitable zone around the sun, which lies beyond the orbit of Venus. Conversely, if a planet does not receive enough sunlight, its oceans may freeze by a process called runaway glaciation. Suppose Earth somehow slipped slightly farther from the sun. As the solar rays faded, the climate would get colder and the polar ice caps would expand. Because snow and ice reflect more sunlight back to space, the climate would become colder still. This vicious cycle could explain in part why Mars, which occupies the next orbit out from Earth, is frozen today.

The actual story of Mars is probably more complicated. Pictures taken from the *Mariner* and *Viking* probes and from the *Global Surveyor* spacecraft show that older parts of the Martian surface are laced with channels carved by liquid water. Measurements from the laser altimeter on board the *Global Surveyor* indicate that the vast northern plains of Mars are exceptionally flat. The only correspondingly smooth surfaces on Earth lie on the seafloor, far from the midocean ridges. Thus, many scientists are now even more confident that Mars once had an ocean. Mars, it would seem, orbits within a potentially habitable zone around the sun. But somehow, eons ago, it plunged into its current chilly state.

A Once Faint Sun

Understanding that dramatic change on Mars may help explain nagging questions about the ancient oceans of Earth. Theories of solar evolution predict that when the sun first became stable, it was 30 percent dimmer than it is now. The smaller solar output would have caused the oceans to be completely frozen before about two billion years ago. But the geologic record tells a different tale: liquid water and life were both present as early as 3.8 billion years ago. The disparity between this prediction and fossil evidence has been termed the faint young sun paradox.

150

The paradox disappears only when one recognizes that the composition of the atmosphere has changed considerably over time. The early atmosphere probably contained much more carbon dioxide than at present and perhaps more methane. Both these gases enhance the greenhouse effect because they absorb infrared radiation; their presence could have kept the early Earth warm, despite less heat coming from the sun.

The greenhouse phenomenon also helps to keep Earth's climate in a dynamic equilibrium through a process called the carbonate-silicate cycle. Volcanoes continually belch carbon dioxide into the atmosphere. But silicate minerals on the continents absorb much of this gas as they erode from crustal rocks and wash out to sea. The carbon dioxide then sinks to the bottom of the ocean in the form of solid calcium carbonate. Over millions of years, plate tectonics drives this carbonate down into the upper mantle, where it reacts chemically and is spewed out as carbon dioxide again through volcanoes.

If Earth had ever suffered a global glaciation, silicate rocks, for the most part, would have stopped eroding. But volcanic carbon dioxide would have continued to accumulate in the atmosphere until the greenhouse effect became large enough to melt the ice. And eventually the warmed oceans would have released enough moisture to bring on heavy rains and to speed erosion, in the process pulling carbon dioxide out of the atmosphere and out of minerals. Thus, Earth has a built-in thermostat that automatically maintains its surface temperature within the range of liquid water.

Paul Hoffman and Daniel Schrag of Harvard University have argued that Earth did freeze over at least twice during the Late Precambrian era, 600 to 750 million years ago. Earth recovered with a buildup of volcanic carbon dioxide. This theory remains controversial because scientists do not fully understand how the biota would have survived, but I am convinced it happened. There is no other good way to explain the evidence for continental-scale, low-latitude glaciation. Six hundred million years ago, Australia straddled the equator, and it was glaciated from one end to the other.

The same mechanism may have operated on Mars. Although the planet is now volcanically inactive, it once had many eruptions and could have maintained a vigorous carbonate-silicate cycle. If Mars has sufficient stores of carbon—one question that NASA scientists hope to answer with the Global Surveyor—it could also have had a dense shroud of carbon dioxide at one time. Clouds of carbon dioxide ice, which scatter infrared radiation, and perhaps a small amount of methane would have generated enough greenhouse heating to maintain liquid water on the surface.

Mars is freeze-dried today not because it is too far from the sun but because it is a small planet and therefore cooled off comparatively quickly. It was unable to sustain the volcanism necessary to maintain balmy temperatures. Over the eons, the water ice that remained probably mixed with dust and is now trapped in the uppermost few kilometers of the Martian crust.

The conditions on Earth that formed and maintain the oceans—an orbit in the habitable zone, plate tectonics creating ocean basins, volcanism driving a carbonate-silicate cycle, and a stratified atmosphere that prevents loss of water or hydrogen—are unique among the planets in our solar system. But other planets are known to orbit other stars, and the odds are good that similar conditions may prevail, creating other brilliantly blue worlds, with oceans much like ours.

Earth has been continuously bombarded by debris since the solar system first formed. Early on, the leftovers colliding with the planets were the size of planets themselves. Large collisions are the probable explanation behind solar system oddities like the rotation of Venus, which is opposite of the other planets' rotations, and the creation of Earth's moon. The record of many smaller impacts over the past 4.5 billion years can be seen on the cratered surfaces of the Moon and Mercury.

Today, more than 100 tons of space debris collide with Earth daily, mostly specks of dust or sometimes rice-sized bits that leave behind meteor trails as they burn up in the atmosphere. Occasionally, a chunk is large enough to survive the trip through the *atmosphere and reach the ground intact or in pieces. These small meteorites have injured people and damaged property.*

But the solar system still contains many asteroids and comets, and the threat of a large impact remains. Once every 100 million years or so, Earth collides with an asteroid or comet large enough to influence climate around the globe. The most recent such event probably occurred 65 million years ago, leading to the extinction of the dinosaurs and the rise of mammalian life on Earth.

In "Target Earth," David Morrison explores how life on Earth can be affected by the solar debris that crosses Earth's path. —EM

"Target Earth"
by David Morrison
Astronomy, February 2002

In June 1908, an alien visitor encountered Earth over the vast forests of Siberia. Shrouded in flames, this visitor—a meteorite—arced across the sky, leaving a trail of dirty smoke. Residents of the small villages along the newly completed Trans-Siberian Railroad gazed at the apparition in wonder. Meanwhile, the celestial interloper headed north over even more desolate wilderness, exploding before reaching the ground.

The resulting airburst, at an estimated altitude of five miles (eight kilometers), flattened more than six hundred square miles (about a thousand square kilometers) of forest near the Stony Tunguska River. Experts believe the explosion released 15 megatons of energy. Seismometers recorded the shock wave, and sensitive microbarographs detected the atmospheric pressure wave around the globe. The following night in England a strange glow suffused the northern sky, so bright that people could read newspapers at midnight.

The Tunguska event is now recognized as a collision of Earth with a stony asteroid, nearly 200 feet (60 meters) in diameter. Scientists use data from Tunguska to calibrate an understanding of terrestrial impact hazards. Together with the much larger dinosaur-killing impact of 65 million years ago, the Siberian event serves as a benchmark of the hazards associated with cosmic collisions.

Had the Tunguska projectile struck near a city, it would rank among the world's most well-known natural disasters. However, because water covers three-fourths of the world's surface and much of the land area is sparsely inhabited like Siberia, few asteroid impacts would result in the destruction of a city with millions of casualties. If the Tunguska event had taken place in an ocean, or if the new seismic and pressure instruments had not been running, no record would exist.

The Tunguska impact remained a unique event in the century that followed. Therefore, it's easy to imagine that if Tunguska had exploded over an ocean, even today scientists might not recognize the impact hazard posed by asteroids. That leaves the dilemma of treating the Tunguska impact as a fluke, or anticipating another catastrophic asteroid impact. Some answers may lie in the moon's cratering record.

If the Tunguska asteroid had hit the airless moon instead, it would have exploded at the surface and excavated a crater a little over a half-mile (one kilometer) across. The moon shows evidence of thousands of similar impact craters of varying sizes. Roughly 17 percent of the lunar surface was resurfaced by volcanic flows about 3.5 billion years ago—after the period of heavy bombardment ended. Because scientists know the age of the dark lava flows of the lunar maria, they can count those craters and estimate average impact rates. Planetary geologist Gene Shoemaker, considered the father of impact studies, first made this calculation nearly two decades ago. He estimated that a Tunguska-size (15 megaton) impact should occur somewhere on Earth about once per century, on average. For such a rare event, it's not surprising that, at most, only a few ambiguous historical (and mythical) possibilities—but no authenticated records—exist.

By taking Shoemaker's conclusion about lunar craters and using much smaller and more frequent impact events, scientists can extrapolate an independent estimate of Earth's current impact rate. As my colleague Clark Chapman (of the Southwest Research Institute in Boulder, Colorado) and I realized a decade ago, the same arguments that predict a Tunguska-type impact once per century lead us to expect an impact with the energy of the Hiroshima atomic bomb (15 kilotons) about once or twice per year. At first encounter, this seems like an obvious contradiction: If an explosion the size of an atomic bomb occurred every few months, print and visual media would report them.

To resolve this paradox, look at what happens to incoming projectiles. The smaller the object, the higher in the atmosphere it decelerates and explodes. A projectile with the energy of the Hiroshima bomb explodes so far above the surface that people are unaware of the event unless they happen to be looking. Meteoroids the size of the Tunguska projectile explode in the lower atmosphere. Only the largest projectiles make it to the ground at a high speed, blasting out craters.

This still does not verify whether 15-kiloton explosions are occurring in the upper atmosphere every few months. Fortunately, there is a way to test this prediction. For the past quarter century, the military and intelligence agencies of the United States and Russia have been monitoring Earth from orbit, looking for rocket launches or clandestine nuclear tests. Military surveillance satellites observe the entire planet, which means that the full global area of Earth serves as a meteor detector.

During the Cold War, these data were classified. We now know, however, that the military and intelligence agencies were fully aware that they were detecting large meteor events. They saw the meteors, determined that they posed no national security danger, and promptly discarded most of the observations. Now, every few months the U.S. Air Force issues a press release on detection of large meteors.

On February 1, 1994, half a dozen satellites over the Western Pacific tracked a large meteor's plunge through the atmosphere using visible and infrared cameras. The incoming rock broke into several pieces, with the largest descending to an altitude of 13 miles (21 km) before exploding. The total energy was estimated at 50 to 100 kilotons, several times larger than that released over Hiroshima. Because the entry took place over open ocean, there were few witnesses and no possibility of collecting any meteorite fragments. Later, Micronesian fishermen reported seeing the final explosion, which they described as "brighter than the sun."

Space data confirm that Earth is currently being bombarded at about the same rate as Shoemaker had deduced from lunar cratering. At least one 15-kiloton atmospheric explosion occurs annually. It therefore follows that the estimate for Tunguska-size impacts is also correct, at roughly one per century.

In order to estimate the risk level from impacts of this size and frequency, scientists note that there are no extended global effects from such an explosion; only people and creatures near the impact site are at risk.

Paradoxically, when considering meteoroid impacts, rare events cause more concern than smaller, more frequent impacts. Although the danger of dying as the result of a Tunguska-size impact is very small, the risk increases dramatically with the increasing size of the asteroid: This is because casualties rise at a disproportionately faster rate than the frequency of a larger projectile hitting Earth drops off. While large impacts are exceedingly rare, the fact is that most of the risk is associated with them, and not with the smaller, Tunguska-class impacts.

Of all life-threatening natural or human-caused risks, cosmic impacts represent the extreme combination of very low probability with very high consequences per event.

Likewise, open-ocean impact results prove fodder for another intriguing set of statistical data. Immediate blast effects of an ocean strike are nil, unless an unlucky ship happens to be near the point of impact. The energy of an open-ocean explosion dissipates differently than on land. A meteor impact would produce a large transient cavity that refills instantly as surrounding ocean water rushes to refill it. This sloshing back and forth generates a tidal wave, or tsunami, which propagates outward like the expanding ripples in a pool. As it travels for thousands of miles, the tsunami efficiently transports part of the impact energy across large distances, making the radius of destruction from the expanding tsunami much greater than that from an explosion on land.

An open-ocean tsunami is not dangerous. While the tsunami wave itself is very large, the ocean is very deep, and a nearby ship may not even notice the effects caused at the surface. As the tsunami approaches land, however, the giant wave encounters friction with the shelving sea bottom and grows in height. When the wave breaks and penetrates inland, it towers over the landscape, causing enormous damage and placing coastal populations at risk.

Throughout the world, population centers develop along shorelines or on river estuaries, where there is ready access to fishing and marine commerce. It's a trend that accelerated in the past century, and now more than half of the world's largest cities are on an ocean coast. This population distribution enhances the destructive potential of tsunami.

Little information exists on the formation of a tsunami by an explosion or of the effects when an extremely large tsunami reaches the land. Large tsunami are rare, and those studied originated in undersea earthquakes or landslides—not celestial impacts. Impacts must be larger than the explosion over Tunguska in order to generate a tsumani dangerous enough to affect coastal areas. Such impacts, by asteroids or even comets hundreds of meters in diameter, are exceedingly rare, probably not more than once in tens of thousands of years. The tsunami risk is therefore more difficult to quantify than the risk associated with Tunguska-class impacts on land.

Computational modeling of impacts indicates that there is a threshold size of about one million megatons of energy beyond which the effects of an impact become global. This energy corresponds to an asteroid size of between one and two kilometers (just over half a mile to one-and-a-quarter miles) in diameter.

Above this threshold, the entire planet is subject to environmental perturbations, primarily from dust blasted into the stratosphere.

As crops fail around the globe, the individual risk goes up as well. Your chance of dying from such a global-scale impact is roughly 100 times greater than from a Tunguska-class impact. In addition, global catastrophes threaten the stability of civilization itself; that is why scientific and public interest focuses on these larger impacts. And that is also why astronomers are actively surveying the sky to find all of the near-Earth asteroids larger than one kilometer in diameter. Today they are more than halfway to achieving this goal, thanks to the Spaceguard Survey.

Funded mostly by NASA, the international Spaceguard Survey discovers about 25 new NEAs (near-Earth asteroids) monthly using specially designed telescopes. Although relatively small (about one meter in aperture), these telescopes are equipped with the most advanced CCD detectors and computers to analyze the data, finding faint moving asteroids against the background of millions of stationary stars.

None of the roughly 1,500 NEAs found so far, including the 530 larger than one kilometer, poses any danger of striking Earth over at least the next century. As the survey progresses, we will eventually eliminate the risk of an unexpected impact from a large asteroid, but the current survey is far from complete at the smaller size NEAs.

Chances are, no comet or asteroid will damage Earth any time soon; however, scientists want to predict the future and prepare in case the unexpected happens. Although we often discuss impact statistics, the situation is actually deterministic. There either is or is not an impact that will take place during our lifetimes.

The challenge for astronomers is not to calculate the statistics, but to go out and discover the next impactor before it hits us unawares.

The Beginnings of Life

6

The water molecule, H_2O, is now known to be much more common in the universe than was once believed. In fact, we have found water elsewhere in the solar system: permanently frozen in the polar caps of Mars, covering the crust of Jupiter's moon Europa, and orbiting the Sun as the primary ingredient of comets. As we currently understand it, life—even the forms of it found in Earth's extreme environments—relies on water.

Scientists are now finding that the water molecule is everywhere in the universe. Water is found in vapor form, often residing with organic molecules in clouds of interstellar gas. Organic molecules, which contain carbon atoms, combine to form amino acids. Amino acids have also been found in both interstellar clouds and in rare and fragile meteorites, called carbonaceous chondrites, left over from the formation of the solar system. Amino acids in turn link in chains to

*make proteins, the building blocks of life,
which have yet to be found outside Earth. In
short, the universe is filled with the chemistry
needed for life. When conditions are right, as
they were around the forming Sun and on
the early Earth, these ingredients must make the
transition to life. —EM*

"Searching for the Molecules of Life in Space"
by Steve Nadis
Sky & Telescope, January 2002

Flying in formation in solar orbit a million miles from
home, the four linked telescopes of NASA's Terrestrial
Planet Finder (TPF) methodically scan star after star
within a range of 50 light-years of Earth. Their collec-
tive mission is to discover planets, ideally Earth-size
planets, orbiting stars like the Sun. As it finds them, the
TPF's spectroscope scrutinizes each new world, searching for signs of water vapor, carbon dioxide, ozone, and
methane—the chemical signatures of life.

While this scenario may seem futuristic, both
NASA and the European Space Agency (ESA) are
actively planning (albeit separately) for such a mission.
Although both missions are technologically complex,
their launch sometime during the next decade is not
beyond the realm of possibility.

But we don't have to wait 10 years or more to
begin searching for the molecules of life. The quest, in

fact, is already under way with more modest space observatories probing the interstellar clouds from which stars and planets form, to see if they contain life's essential ingredients.

Chemistry in Space

"Almost everything we see in galaxies emerges from molecular clouds, which is why these regions are of intrinsic interest," explains Gary J. Melnick of the Harvard-Smithsonian Center for Astrophysics (CfA). "The question we seek to answer is whether there are processes going on all around us that suggest the conditions in our solar system are not unique."

That question hinges, to a large degree, on chemistry—particularly that involving water. Every atom, molecule, and ion has a unique spectral signature, a set of lines in the electromagnetic spectrum produced when it radiates energy. This fact can be exploited to study the chemistry of interstellar space. For example, after colliding with other atoms and molecules in a nebulas water can radiate at thousands of different wavelengths depending on the temperature and density of the cloud it inhabits. Ideally, astronomers would like to see all the spectral lines emitted by this radiation but they can make a positive identification of water, and try to estimate its abundance, by seeing just one line.

The strategy of identifying elements by their characteristic emissions has been used during the past few decades to spot more than 120 molecules in interstellar space. Some, like hydrogen, were found with

Earth-based infrared telescopes and a few with optical instruments, but the majority have been observed in the radio spectrum where molecules emit most of their energy.

The View from Orbit

Until recently we had no way of unambiguously detecting water and oxygen, two common molecules closely associated with life on Earth. Carbon dioxide, oxygen, and water vapor in our atmosphere absorb and emit copious amounts of infrared and submillimeter radiation, obscuring the weak emissions coming from space. The best way to overcome this problem is to send an observatory into orbit. So far two satellites have been launched to search for cosmic clouds of water and oxygen: the Infrared Space Observatory (ISO), operated by ESA from November 1995 until May 1998, and the submillimeter Wave Astronomy Satellite (SWAS), which reached orbit in December 1998 (*S&T*: April 1999, page 28) and will continue operations possibly until 2004.

Although the ISO mission ended more than three years ago, scientific findings are still emerging from its archival data. "We saw more than 20 molecules that were detected in space for the first time, including the ring-shaped benzene, which is considered a stepping-stone for the formation of more complex organic molecules," says Martin Kessler, ISO's project scientist from 1984 to 2001. "We also observed several hundred transitions of water, one of the key molecules of life, and found it everywhere we looked." Vast quantities of water vapor were seen in star-forming regions like those in the Orion Nebula, where it is being produced at a rate that would fill Earth's oceans once every 24 minutes. "Most of the water on Earth was created by these giant factories in space," Kessler adds. ISO also detected water in galaxies, as well as in the giant planets and comets of our solar system.

While ISO looked at relatively "warm" water in the 100° to 200° Kelvin (-279° to -99° F) range, SWAS focuses on cold clouds, 10° to 200° above absolute zero (0° Kelvin), which represent the bulk of material in interstellar space. Although it studied many of the same regions, ISO was more sensitive to the hot spots localized around stars, whereas SWAS is more sensitive to the colder zones spread out over a much wider area. Moreover, SWAS, with narrower wavelength coverage than ISO, can see just one water spectral line at 0.54 millimeter. This is the lowest transition of water that occurs when a molecule in its ground state is hit by a hydrogen atom, starts to spin, and releases energy in the form of distinctive submillimeter-wave radiation.

Water, Water Everywhere

To date SWAS has inspected comets; the atmospheres of Mars, Jupiter, and Saturn; and about 120 molecular clouds selected largely on the basis of their interesting radio characteristics. Like ISO, SWAS found "water, water everywhere," says Melnick, the mission's principal investigator.

The fact that water is so prevalent in interstellar clouds is reassuring to Christopher F. Chyba, a planetary scientist at the SETI Institute in Mountain View, California. "If you see water everywhere, as we do, that's at least a hint that it's broadly available to serve as a medium to support life, assuming the conditions exist to keep it in a liquid state?" Life as we know it depends on liquid water, organic (carbon-bearing) molecules, and an energy source such as a star—requirements that, based on the latest evidence, may not be so hard to satisfy.

The presence—and indeed the ubiquity—of water may help explain one of the great mysteries in astronomy: how stars form. As giant clouds of gas and dust collapse under the pull of gravity, the gas heats up and wants to expand. But the gas must somehow cool itself so that the collapse and eventual birth of a star can proceed. "The way we think nature solves the problem is through collisions within clouds, which result in the excitation of molecules and atoms to higher energy levels," explains Melnick. When molecules such as water are excited in this way, they rid themselves of energy by emitting radiation at specific wavelengths, which is precisely what SWAS has seen. By zeroing in on water's lowest transition state, it provides clues about the early stages of cloud collapse.

A Question of Quantity

Although SWAS continues to find water everywhere it looks, there doesn't seem to be enough to satisfy most models of star and planet formation. The water SWAS has observed in cold clouds is only 0.1 to 1 percent as abundant as predicted. Gaseous oxygen is also astonishingly scarce, and, in fact, SWAS has not detected any molecular oxygen to date. "We know that stars form from the collapse of these clouds," Melnick says. "But as to the next step—what happens chemically when the clouds begin to collapse—we're finding the conventional view is not correct." Without ample quantities of water in these clouds, another coolant is required. Carbon monoxide is now believed to dominate at low temperatures, whereas water vapor takes over during the collapse when temperatures exceed 300° Kelvin.

The SWAS team has already devised a scenario to explain the low water counts, concluding that more water is frozen onto dust grains than anticipated. Ice-coated dust gives off infrared radiation, but at wavelengths invisible to the satellite's instruments.

The dearth of oxygen is harder to explain, because these molecules are not likely to be cloaked by dust grains. "There are no observational signs of frozen oxygen, so there is no easy out available to us," says Cornell astronomer Paul Goldsmith, a SWAS team member. Recent ISO findings suggest that, contrary to current thinking, more oxygen may reside in atomic form (which SWAS's instruments can't detect) than in molecular form.

The ostensible shortage of water and oxygen, says Goldsmith, "might be a hint that something is wrong with our picture of the structure of these giant clouds." He was initially disappointed by the results, as they suggested a big gap between existing theories and the first observations of this kind ever made. But upon reflection, he says, "In some sense it's much more interesting when your observations contradict prevailing wisdom."

While the standard theory appears to be off in several crucial details, the general picture is not entirely shaken. "If our interpretation is correct," Melnick observes, "water is not a rare species; apparently, it's just rare in the gaseous phase." The implications, if confirmed, are profound. "SWAS shows that the most fundamental ingredient of life is not isolated," he says. "It's widespread and may be present in sufficient quantity to support systems analogous to our solar system."

Water and Earth

Further investigation by SWAS, and future experiments on other spacecraft, could help us understand where oceans come from, says Melnick. "If planets like Earth are formed from the debris left after stars are made, the oceans could be partly due to the release of water from ice-coated grains." These grains might also clump together to form the comets that later rained down on Earth.

Exactly how the water in Earth's oceans got here is still "the weakest link in our theory," according to Cornell astronomer Martin Harwit, a member of both the ISO and SWAS science teams. There are two main possibilities: water could have been tied up in the rocks that made up Earth, or comets and asteroids could have carried it here. Melnick considers both scenarios plausible. "If water is present in the diffuse medium, it's not such a stretch to think it could make its way into bodies that form from the collapse of this medium."

Comets, which are about 50 percent water, can transport tanker-loads of the substance, and impacts from comets are thought to have been more frequent early in Earth's history. For example, in 1994 Comet Shoemaker-Levy 9 dumped 2 million tons of water onto Jupiter. ISO scientists calculate that one impact every millennium during Earth's first billion years would have provided enough water to fill the oceans and lakes.

Impacts by asteroids were also more frequent in the past, although these rocky bodies contain at most 10 percent water. But recent computer simulations (*S&T:* February 2001, page 26) suggest that asteroids may have played a more important role in supplying Earth's water than previously believed.

By extending their survey to a couple hundred regions scattered throughout the galaxy, SWAS astronomers hope to gain a better grasp of the water-abundance measurements and test the theory that water is frozen on grains. "The only way to test this idea is to look at regions with different conditions—different densities and temperatures—to see what the [water] shortfall really is," says Edwin A. Bergin, a SWAS investigator at the CfA.

Another strategy employed by the team is to study environments where no water is expected and see what they find. So-called "carbon stars" are a good example. Melnick and his colleagues used SWAS to look at IRC + 10216 (CW Leonis), a carbon store located about 500 light-years from Earth. Having exhausted the supply of hydrogen and helium in its core, CW Leonis is in the late stages of stellar evolution. Carbon produced in the star's center is dredged up to the surface, where it latches on to oxygen to form carbon monoxide. "In this kind of environment, you wouldn't expect to find water, because carbon will snatch up oxygen leaving little available to form H_2O," Melnick explains.

But SWAS found the star's water to be 10,000 times more abundant than predicted (*S&T*: October 2001, page 26). After ruling out alternative theories, he and his collaborators surmise that as CW Leonis increases in size and luminosity, hundreds of billions of icy bodies orbiting the star in a belt of comets similar to the Sun's Kuiper Belt are gradually vaporizing, releasing vast quantities of water. This is the first time that astronomers have detected water around another star that appears to be linked to comets, says Melnick. "If we're right, it means the architecture of our solar system is not unique."

Looking into the Future

To follow up on this work, astronomers obviously want to look at other carbon stars. "That's hard for SWAS to do, since this detection took 400 hours of telescope time," Melnick admits. "But it could be left for future missions." The Herschel Space Observatory (HSO), a 3.5-meter telescope that ESA plans to launch in 2007, could explore far-infrared and sub-millimeter wavelengths more thoroughly and efficiently than SWAS. The spectrometers on HSO will be able to look at more spectral lines of water and other elements.

Together with the Stratospheric Observatory for Infrared Astronomy, a 2.5-meter telescope installed in a Boeing 7475P aircraft and due to begin operations in 2004, HSO will hasten the search for the molecules of life. Looking farther into the future, NASA's Terrestrial Planet Finder and Darwin, an almost identical European mission that may ultimately merge with it, offer a quantum leap forward in this pursuit. "While we're studying the haystack, trying to draw the bigger picture, they'll be going after the needle itself," says ESA's Kessler. TPF and Darwin are being designed to discover Earth-like planets; determine their size, temperature, and position with respect to the parent star; and see if their atmospheres betray any hints of life. The technical challenge will be immense, as each telescope in the TPF array will be separated from its companions by perhaps a kilometer. According to Harwit, that baseline will need to be maintained, ideally, to within a fraction of the wavelength of light being studied.

A further difficulty in searching for signs of life is that it's hard to know what to look for. "Life on Earth involves water vapor, oxygen, and carbon dioxide, which is what we'd probably start with, but we still don't know how life formed here," Harwit says. "We ought to be ready for surprises, since there might be other chemistries we haven't imagined yet."

Our definition of "life" has expanded significantly in the past few decades with the discovery of microbes in "extreme" terrestrial environments previously considered unsuitable for life. Bacteria have been found living in superheated water near geothermal ocean vents and kilometers beneath Earth's crust. These discoveries have raised hopes that similar microbes are living (or may have once lived) in the seemingly inhospitable deserts of Mars or in oceans beneath the icy surface of Jupiter's moon Europa.

These microbes survive without oxygen, an ability that would be necessary for any life found away from the green, oxygenated surface of Earth. Scientists believe that the earliest life on Earth probably flourished in environments without oxygen. In addition, these microbes live in the complete absence of sunlight.

In this article, Paul Davies, a professor of natural philosophy at the Australian Centre for Astrobiology at Macquarie University in Sydney, explores the possibilities for life outside of Earth based on what we now know about life on this planet. —EM

174

"New Hope for Life Beyond Earth"
by Paul Davies
Sky & Telescope, June 2004

Imagine a visitor from space going into orbit about planet Earth and observing its surface. There would be abundant evidence that our planet is swarming with life: atmospheric oxygen produced by plants and algae, chlorophyll in the spectrum, changing patterns of vegetation, and the conspicuous effects of human activity. What would be less obvious, even with sophisticated equipment, is that the biosphere extends deep beneath the surface. Indeed, according to some scientists, there may be as much biomass lurking inside our planet as there is atop it.

Belief in some sort of inhabited underworld is as old as human culture and remains an abiding myth even today. It has proved the stimulus to science fiction stories from Jules Verne's classic *Journey to the Center of the Earth* to Robin Cook's recent novel *Abduction*. Alas, the reality is more prosaic than the fantasy. There are no monsters lurking vast cavernous spaces, no hidden civilizations—just microbes dwelling in tiny rock pores. Yet the existence of these real-life denizens of the underworld has far-reaching scientific consequences and is transforming the prospects for finding life on other bodies in our solar system and beyond.

Life Below Earth

The first hint that life on Earth is not restricted to the near surface came in the early 1970s when the research submarine Alvin explored a system of volcanic vents on the floor of the Pacific Ocean. Biologists were amazed to see a variety of organisms living near the vents, in total darkness, and at enormous pressures. These creatures included weird varieties of crabs, clams, and tubeworms. Stranger still, Alvin discovered colonies of microbes living off the scalding effluent that spews from the vents. These hardy organisms are known as hyperthermophiles because of their extraordinary heat tolerance. Some thrive in temperatures above the normal boiling point of water. (Because of the high pressure, water at that depth doesn't boil at 100° C.) Furthermore, since sunlight cannot penetrate to the bottom of the ocean, photosynthesis isn't possible. Instead, these primary producers use thermal and chemical energy to survive.

If subsurface life were restricted to pockets surrounding volcanic vents on the seabed, it would be little more than an exotic curiosity. But Alvin's discovery turned out to be just the tip of the iceberg. A few years later Cornell astrophysicist Thomas Gold, best known for his pioneering work on pulsars, persuaded the Swedish government to back a controversial drilling project. Gold had a theory that gas and oil might be sheltered beneath slabs of granite. While that idea remains highly contentious, the borehole drilled in the remote forests of Sweden did turn up something important: traces of organisms living several kilometers deep in the Earth's crust.

At first Gold's claim to have found signs of life so far underground was greeted with skepticism and even outright hostility. Colleagues were openly scornful, and

Gold had trouble getting his results published. But by the mid-1990s several other research groups were finding microbes a kilometer or so deep too. In particular, boreholes drilled in the Columbia River region of Washington yielded a rich harvest of organisms, some of which were extracted and cultured in the laboratory.

About the same time, the International Ocean Drilling Project was recovering rock samples from nearly a kilometer beneath the seabed that were literally seething with microbes. It began to seem as if microbial life pervades the Earth's subsurface to a depth of some kilometers. Because temperature rises with depth due to Earth's internal heat, these deep-living organisms are also mostly thermophiles or hyperthermophiles. While it is too soon to say how extensive this deep, hot biosphere may be, it is clearly widespread, and its existence must be factored into the story of life.

Gene sequencing has enabled microbiologists to position these subterranean microbes on the tree of life. Significantly, the oldest and deepest branches of the tree are occupied by hyperthermophiles. The heat-loving subsurface organisms are living fossils, representing an extremely ancient lineage. They continue a lifestyle that may have remained largely unchanged for billions of years.

Some scientists see this as a pointer to how life began, suggesting that the first organisms dwelt in the hot, deep subsurface, where they were protected from the intense cometary and asteroidal bombardment that pounded the planets until about 3.8 billion years ago. The largest impacts would have released enough energy to swathe the Earth in incandescent rock vapor, boiling the oceans and sending a sterilizing beat pulse into the crust to a depth of at least a kilometer. Yet there would have existed a "Goldilocks zone" for hyperthermophiles in the crust of the ancient Earth, deep enough to avoid incineration by cosmic impacts, but not so deep that the geothermal heat would prove lethal.

An important question for astrobiologists is whether subsurface ecosystems can be fully self-sustaining. Many deep-living microbes depend indirectly on surface life, either feeding on organic molecules that descend from above or requiring traces of photosynthetically produced oxygen to metabolize. However, some microbes, called chemotrophs, are known to survive on inorganic gases and minerals without any assistance from the products of surface life.

For example, when water permeates hot rocks deep underground, it can become dissociated into hydrogen and oxygen. The dissolved hydrogen, together with carbon dioxide, can serve as an energy source for metabolism, and some microbes can utilize these chemicals by converting them into methane gas. In theory, such "methanogens" could support an independent food chain, enabling a subsurface ecosystem to endure in the absence of any surface life at all.

As long as scientists believed that biology required sunlight as well as liquid water, the prospects for finding life beyond Earth were severely limited. But with the discovery of subsurface life flourishing on Earth, the possibilities for life elsewhere are greatly enhanced.

Life Beyond Earth

Take Europa, a moon of Jupiter. Space probes show a body completely covered with a thick layer of ice. But Europa has an internal heat supply, in the form of tidal friction. As Europa orbits the giant planet, it bends and flexes due to the continuously changing gravitational tug of war between it, its sister moons, and Jupiter. This flexing produces a steady heat source capable of melting water ice in the interior of the moon. Indeed, observations suggest that beneath Europa's icy crust there is a substantial liquid water ocean. Photosynthetic life is ruled out below the ice because of the complete lack of sunlight—but chemotrophic life may still be possible. Opinions differ about how far Europan life might have evolved. Probably it would be confined to microbes clustering around hot vents on the ocean floor. Yet some optimists have painted a picture of rich marine life swimming in the pitch-black subsurface sea.

The realistic prospects for finding life beneath Europa's icy crust, or in the proposed underground saltwater oceans of Ganymede and Callisto, remain uncertain until astronomers get a better sense of what the Jovian moons are made of, how they formed and evolved, and what their radiation and space-weathering environments truly are. These questions are the driving force behind NASA's proposed Jupiter Icy Moons Orbiter (JIMO). This nuclear-powered craft, slated to launch no earlier than 2011, will use ion-propulsion engines to visit the three moons in turn, paving the way for eventual Jovian-system landers in the distant future.

The knowledge of organisms deep below ground has also given added hope to the chances of finding traces of life on Mars. In the first few hundred million years of the solar system, Mars was probably more hospitable to life than Earth. Its main advantage concerns its rate of cooling. All the planets started out intensely hot, but Earth was doubly afflicted. As our planet was first cooling, a Mars-size body plowed into it, forming the Moon and melting Earth in the process. Despite constant bombardment by primordial solar-system flotsam and asteroid-belt strays, the smaller red planet had the chance to cool before Earth, opening up an earlier opportunity for subsurface life. Comfortably ensconced beneath a kilometer or two of rock, microbes on early Mars could have withstood the worst of the bombardment and thrived at a time when Earth's crust was still lethally hot.

Later, life may have been possible on the Martian surface. Evidence from spacecraft suggests a warm, wet Martian epoch. Some even speculate that Mars once had enough water to cover the planet with a 1-km-deep ocean (*S&T*: August 2003, page 30). The recent finding by the Opportunity rover proving that parts of Mars were indeed soaked with water (May issue, page 44) strongly backs up that claim.

Once the intense bombardment abated, near-surface and even surface life may have evolved on Mars, taking advantage of meandering rivers, volcanic vents in shallow lakes, and gurgling springs on the sides of volcanoes. All this came to an end when the atmosphere leaked away, sending the surface temperature plummeting and transforming an ancient paradise into the freeze-dried desert we see today

The prospects for finding any sort of extant life on Mars are slim but perhaps not totally hopeless. From what we know about terrestrial life in extreme environments, one should not completely rule out some sort of hardy microbial subsurface life on Mars. Estimates of the Martian heat flow suggest that the planet's internal temperature is sufficient to melt the permafrost a kilometer or two below the surface, creating some briny aquifers that could, in principle, host the sort of bacteria that lurk deep within Earth's crust. Candidates include methanogens, making a living from hydrogen or hydrogen sulphide and exuding methane gas as a byproduct. Britain's *Beagle 2* lander, which formed part of the European Space Agency's Mars Express mission, was specifically designed to sniff out telltale traces of methane that might have percolated to the surface. With the loss *Beagle 2*, we shall have to await future missions before sting this hypothesis further. If microbes are clinging on for survival below the Martian surface today, they might be remnant of the earliest form of life there, or they could present the last remaining vestiges of a once-flourishing surface biota, which retreated belowground and adapted to subsurface living when the red planet froze.

These developments also carry important implications for extrasolar life. Astrobiologists traditionally defined the "habitable zone" around stars as the distance at which an orbiting planet might sustain liquid water on its surface for extended durations. The conventional habitable zone round the Sun, for example, extends from somewhere between the orbits of Venus and Earth out about as far as Mars. The precise extent of a habitable zone depends on the mass of the star, where it is in its evolutionary cycle, and assumptions about planetary atmospheres.

Subsurface life implies that planetary systems may possess more than one habitable zone. Giant planets are likely to have moons, like Europa, large enough to undergo significant tidal friction, elevating the temperature above the freezing point of water even when they are located far from the star. Indeed, it is possible to contemplate moons with subsurface life orbiting rogue giant planets that have been flung out of their planetary systems or born as orphans and left to wander me dark interstellar spaces (*S&T*: November 2002, page 38).

Life in Transit

The discovery that microbes dwell happily deep in apparently solid rock gives credence to the theory that life can be transported between planets inside material blasted into space by big impacts. Although the intense early bombardment finished long ago, Mars and Earth still take a big bit from time to time. Every few million years, one of these impacts will pack enough punch to splatter debris through interplanetary pace. Calculations by H. Jay Melosh and his colleagues at the University of

Arizona indicate that a substantial fraction of the ejected material avoids being excessively shock-heated or pulverized and could convey live microbes into space.

Cocooned inside a boulder a couple of meters across a microbial colony could withstand thousands or even millions of years in orbit. Crucially, any radiation would be drastically reduced by the rock's shielding effect. The incumbent organisms would also be spared incineration if the rock were to plunge through the atmosphere of another planet. The cold vacuum of space would oblige the microbes to cease metabolizing, but it would also act as an excellent preservative. We know that Mars and Earth trade rocks on an ongoing basis; it seems likely that they would trade organisms too, if there is—or was—any life on Mars. Similar "transpermic" processes might be expected to operate between nearby planets elsewhere in the universe too, though the chances of an exchange of life between neighboring star systems in this manner are extremely slim.

The origin of life remains a tantalizing mystery. Did the very first organism form in the broiling bosom of the Earth or in the less torrid depths of ancient Mars? Or was it incubated in an entirely different setting—in a balmy, sun-drenched lake, perhaps, during a lucky quiescent interregnum of the bombardment—multiplying and spreading to the deep subsurface only later? Does the genetic record of a hot, deep past indicate a hot, deep origin, or just a genetic bottleneck through which the primeval biosphere was squeezed by later violent impacts?

The answers to these questions will not be forth-coming without a continued effort to search for extreme life on Earth, Mars, and beyond. President George W. Bush's dramatic announcement in January of a future manned mission to Mars will give added impetus to NASA's flourishing astrobiology program. After all, solving the riddle of life's origin—one of the biggest of the big questions of existence—is a central motivation for exploring the solar system. On the way, we may determine whether the cradle of life was akin to the biblical Garden of Eden, or whether life was forged in a location closer to the traditional concept of Hell.

Paul Davies, "New Hope for Life Beyond Earth," *Sky and Telescope*, June 2004. Copyright © 2004 by Sky Publishing Corp. Reproduced with permission of the publisher.

Web Sites

Due to the changing nature of Internet links, the Rosen Publishing Group, Inc. has developed an online list of Web sites related to the subject of this book. This site is updated regularly. Please use this link to access the list:

http://www.rosenlinks.com/cdfa/hlea

For Further Reading

Beatty, J. Kelly, et al. *The New Solar System*. New York, NY: Cambridge University Press, 1998.

Gonzalez, Guillermo, and Jay Wesley Richards. *The Privileged Planet: How Our Place in the Cosmos Is Designed for Discovery*. Washington, DC: Regnery Publishing, Inc., 2004.

Goodstein, David L., and Judith R. Goodstein. *Feynman's Lost Lecture: The Motion of Planets Around the Sun*. New York, NY: W. W. Norton & Company, 1996.

Hancock, Graham. *The Mars Mystery: The Secret Connection Between Earth and the Red Planet*. New York, NY: Three Rivers Press, 1999

Lowman, Paul D., Jr. *Exploring Space, Exploring Earth*. New York, NY: Cambridge University Press, 2002.

Bibliography

Alper, Joe. "It Came from Outer Space." *Astronomy*, November 2002, pp. 36–42.

Battersby, Stephen. "Into the Sphere of Fire." *New Scientist*, August 2, 2003, pp. 30–34.

Bonnell, Dr. Jerry. "A Bad Day in the Milky Way." PBS.org, January 2002. Retrieved November 3, 2004 (http://www.pbs.org/wgbh/nova/gamma/milkyway.html).

Chown, Marcus, "Chaotic Heavens." *New Scientist*, February 28, 2004, p. 32.

Crawford, Ian. "Where Are They?" *Scientific American*, July 2000, pp. 38–44.

Davies, Paul. "New Hope for Life Beyond Earth," *Sky & Telescope*, June 2004, pp. 41–45.

Garlick, Mark A. "The Fate of the Earth." *Sky & Telescope*, October 2002, pp. 30–35.

Garlick, Mark A. "No Place Like Zone." *Astronomy*, August 2002, pp. 44–52.

Kasting, James F. "The Origins of Water on Earth." *Scientific American*, September 2003, pp. 28–34.

Kasting, James F. "When Methane Made Climate." *Scientific American*, July 2004, pp. 78–86.

Lubick, Naomi. "Goldilocks & The Three Planets." *Astronomy*, July 2003, pp. 36–42.

Morrison, David. "Target Earth." *Astronomy*,
    February 2002, pp. 46–52.

Muir, Hazel. "Earth, Wind and Fire." *New Scientist*,
    May 17, 2003, pp. 26–30.

Nadis, Steve. "Searching for the Molecules of Life in
    Space." *Sky & Telescope*, January 2002, pp. 32–37.

Suplee, Curt. "The Sun: Living with a Stormy Star."
    National Geographic, July 2004, pp. 13–33.

Index

About the Editor

Eric Monier wanted to be an astronomer from the time he was six years old. After receiving his Ph.D. from the University of Pittsburgh in 1998, he spent several years as a postdoctoral fellow at Ohio State University. He is now an assistant professor of physics and the planetarium director at SUNY Brockport.

Photo Credits

Front cover (top inset) © Royalty-Free/Corbis; (center left inset) © Digital Vision/Getty Images; (bottom right inset) © Lynette Cook/Science Photo Library (bottom left inset) © Library of Congress Prints and Photographs Division; (background) Brand X Pictures/ Getty Images. Back cover (top) © Photodisc Green/Getty Images; (bottom) © Digital Vision/Getty Images.

Designer: Geri Fletcher; Editor: Nicholas Croce